THE CHURCH OF GOD IN CHRIST PRESIDING BISHOP

Bishop J. Drew Sheard

"A Mission Made Possible"
Zechariah 4:6

Order materials today from the Power for Living Series:

Church Of God In Christ Publishing House
Evangelist Terri Hannett, Executive Director
Evangelist Barachias Irons, Managing Editor
806 East Brooks Road, Memphis, Tennessee 38116
P.O. Box 161330, Memphis, Tennessee 38186
Toll Free: 1-877-746-8578 | Fax: (901) 743-1555
Website: www.cogicpublishinghouse.net
Email: sales@cogicpublishinghouse.net

FROM THE PRESIDING BISHOP'S DESK

Greetings to each of you in the matchless name of our Lord and Savior, Jesus Christ.

We are living in an unprecedented time, a time of uncertainty and unrest. Systemic racism, police brutality, and an everchanging climate. You may ask, where are the answers, and whom can we trust? As Blood washed individuals, we have our hope in Christ and His Word that says, "No Weapon Formed against us Shall prosper". (Isa. 54:17).

Bishop James Whitehead and members of the Review Committee for the Power For Living curriculum have put together an array of Scriptures and Bible topics that will encourage every believer to stand fast in the knowledge that God is yet on the throne and victory is ours through the blood of Jesus Christ.

As we move forward, hold on to His unchanging hand, for His Word is true and His promises are ours to behold.

Be encouraged,

J. Drew Sheard
Presiding Bishop
Eighth in Succession
Church Of God In Christ, Inc.

FROM THE CHAIRMAN OF THE PUBLISHING BOARD

Blessings in the name of the Lord Jesus Christ,

The fact that you are reading this letter indicates that God has blessed you to experience another year. We often transition from one season to the next and sometimes take for granted the privilege God affords us to see a new year, a new season, and a new day. Thank God for 2023.

Last year, I admonished every believer to take the time to examine their lives. I was led by the Lord to ask us to prepare our hearts daily to receive the seed of His word. The seed has no flaws—it is the Word of God; however, we must tend to the soil of our soul so that His Word will germinate, take root, and bring forth fruit. How do we do that? First, we exercise our faith and trust God as we encounter various trials and tribulations. Secondly, we take the time to feed our faith through prayer, fasting, and meditating on the Word of God day and night (Psalms 1:2). Our faith and our hope in Christ Jesus are vital to making sure that the seeds take root in the ground of our inner man.

God is tilling the soil of our hearts, as there are some personal things that we need to receive from the Lord. Thus, there are times when we need to hear a personal word from the Lord, and there are times when we need to know that we can walk on the waters of life. We need to know that the seeds of faith sown in us will sustain us through our storms, so the storms do not develop inside of us. It is the storms that water our faith, which will ultimately bring forth a harvest of joy. We need to know that our faith in God is not in vain. It is time for us to heal inwardly from these two and a half years of the COVID pandemic, and we must seek out God to make us complete on the inside as well as the outside.

To those loyal supporters of our literature, I want to personally thank you for sticking with us in these trying and troubling times. I ask that you continue to pray for the nations of this world. I ask that you pray for the unity of our country and pray for God to manifest Himself in our lives and in our churches in a new way. I ask that the Lord shift the winds of grace and favor in our direction so that we can experience Him as we have never experienced Him before.

God Bless you, and may He keep you,

Bishop Uleses Henderson, Jr.
Chairman of Publishing Board
Churches Of God In Christ Inc.

FROM THE DESK OF THE CHAIRMAN OF MARKETING

Greetings to all of God's people,

As I look back over a few things in my life, I cannot help but take pause to wonder how I managed to come through specific trials and tribulations. As a Born Again Christian, we are taught that it is God who brings us through periods in our lives in which some are of the most difficult. While this is true, we normally leave out the human factors in this equation. The human factors are, while I was going through these periods, I did not put a pause on my worship of God. In other words, before God brought me out, I was still yet worshiping him, I was still yet praising Him for His goodness, and for His grace and mercy alone.

Is there a time in your life that you can remember when your praises and your worship sustained you until God pulled you out of your tribulation? If so, then the additional reason why God was able to bring you through is that God responded to the continual offerings of your praise and your worship to Him. I honestly believe that's why some of us have not made it out! It is because we have removed this concept from our lives; it is praise that gets God's attention, but it is worship that touches His heart, and more importantly, it is worshiping God while going through that shows Him how much we are in love with Him.

As we study God's word this year, let us keep the theme God gave our Presiding Bishop in the forefront of all our endeavors. Regardless of what we may experience the "Mission is Possible". In our most trying times, we should stand firm on the fact that with man it may seem impossible, but with God "all" things are possible. Let us sincerely ask ourselves: Are we giving God the attention that He deserves in our lives? Are we placing God first in every situation? Are we making sure that God is our primary focus and not our secondary focus? While diving into your Sunday School lessons, keep those thoughts in the forefront of your mind; explore inwardly those convictions that you have, and be honest with yourself. Because honesty is the first step to bringing freedom into your lives, and freedom is the first step to giving God expressions of pure praise and pure worship. *John 4:24 AMPC "God is a Spirit (a spiritual being) and those who worship Him must worship Him in spirit and in truth (reality)".*

God Bless you and my heave continue to smile upon you,

Yours for service,

Sandra S. Jones
Chairman, Marketing/Sales
Church Of God In Christ, Publishing Board.

ADULT QUARTERLY

WINTER QUARTER
DECEMBER 2023 • JANUARY • FEBRUARY 2024

Bishop J. Drew Sheard
Presiding Bishop
Church Of God In Christ, Inc.

Bishop Uleses Henderson Jr., Esq.
Chairman, Publishing Board
Church Of God In Christ, Inc.

JESUS' BIRTH PREDICTED

BIBLE BASIS: LUKE 1:26—40

BIBLE TRUTH: Jesus' conception through the Holy Spirit reveals that nothing is impossible for God.

MEMORY VERSE: "And behold, thou shalt conceive in thy womb, and bring forth a son, and shalt call his name JESUS" (Luke 1:31, KJV).

LESSON AIM: By the end of the lesson, we will: REVIEW the foretelling of Jesus' birth; REFLECT on the unexpected and perplexing events of our lives; and DEDICATE ourselves to the purposes of God.

BACKGROUND SCRIPTURES: Psalm 89:1—7 Read and incorporate the insights gained from the Background Scriptures into your study of the lesson

LESSON SCRIPTURE

LUKE 1:26 – 40, KJV

26 And in the sixth month the angel Gabriel was sent from God unto a city of Galilee, named Nazareth,

27 To a virgin espoused to a man whose name was Joseph, of the house of David; and the virgin's name was Mary.

28 And the angel came in unto her, and said, Hail, thou that art highly favoured, the Lord is with thee: blessed art thou among women.

29 And when she saw him, she was troubled at his saying, and cast in her mind what manner of salutation this should be.

30 And the angel said unto her, Fear not, Mary: for thou hast found favour with God.

31 And, behold, thou shalt conceive in thy womb, and bring forth a son, and shalt call his name JESUS.

32 He shall be great, and shall be called the Son of the Highest: and the Lord God shall give unto him the throne of his father David:

33 And he shall reign over the house of Jacob for ever; and of his kingdom there shall be no end.

34 Then said Mary unto the angel, How shall this be, seeing I know not a man?

35 And the angel answered and said unto her, The Holy Ghost shall come upon thee, and the power of the Highest shall overshadow thee: therefore also that holy thing which shall be born of thee shall be called the Son of God.

36 And, behold, thy cousin Elisabeth, she hath also conceived a son in her old age: and this is the sixth month with her, who was called barren.

37 For with God nothing shall be impossible.

38 And Mary said, Behold the handmaid of the Lord; be it unto me according to thy word. And the angel departed from her.

39 And Mary arose in those days, and went into the hill country with haste, into a city of Juda;

40 And entered into the house of Zacharias, and saluted Elisabeth.

BIBLICAL DEFINITIONS

A. Hail (Luke 1:28) *cairay* (Gk.)—To be cheerful, rejoice. A salutation conveying a wish for the welfare of the person addressed (Luke 1:28); continued among our Saxon forefathers in "Joy to you" and "Health to you."

B. Virgin (v. 10) *parthenos* (Gk.)— Either a marriageable maiden or a young married woman, a pure virgin (2 Corinthians 11:2).

LIFE NEED FOR TODAY'S LESSON

AIM: Students will accept that the announcement of Jesus' birth is a fulfillment of God's purpose.

INTRODUCTION

Zacharias and Elisabeth Luke introduces us to two major players—an exceptional, seasoned couple, Zacharias and Elisabeth, who had received the grace of God in large measure. In the time of Herod, king of Judea, there was a priest named Zacharias of the priestly division of Abijah; his wife, Elisabeth, was also a descendant of Aaron. They were upright in the sight of God, observing all the Lord's commandments and regulations blamelessly. But they had no children because Elisabeth was barren, and they were senior citizens (verses 5–7). Infertility can be a disappointment and for some, unbearable stress. In ancient Hebrew culture barrenness was a disgrace— even a punishment. Barrenness carried a moral stigma for in Jewish thinking, it was not the fate of the righteous. Elisabeth called her barrenness her "reproach" (verse 25).

BIBLE LEARNING

AIM: Students will learn that trusting God in impossible situations takes faith and humility.

I. MARY HEARS THE MESSAGE (LUKE 1:26–38)

We have here an account of the mother of our Lord; though we are not to pray to her, we ought to praise God for her. The angel Gabriel who had previously visited Zacharias, now visits Mary. The angel's address, "Hail, thou that art highly favoured . . . blessed are thou among women" (**verse 28**), means Mary was chosen and favored by God to have the honor of birthing the Messiah, something Jewish mothers had long desired. Note who God decided to choose. She was a teenage virgin. She didn't grow up in a royal household. She wasn't from the religious center of life, Jerusalem, but the small town of Nazareth. God chooses the weak things of this world to confound the mighty (see **1 Corinthians 1:27**).

Christ's Birth Announced (verses 26–38)

26 And in the sixth month the angel Gabriel was sent from God unto a city of Galilee, named Nazareth, 27 To a virgin espoused to a man whose name was Joseph, of the house of David; and the virgin's name was Mary. 28 And the angel came in unto her, and said, Hail, thou that art highly favoured, the Lord is with thee: blessed art thou among women. 29 And when she saw him, she was troubled at his saying, and cast in her mind what manner of salutation this should be. 30 And the angel said unto her, Fear not, Mary: for thou hast found favour with God. 31 And, behold, thou shalt conceive in thy womb, and bring forth a son, and shalt call his name Jesus. 32 He shall be great, and shall be called the

Son of the Highest: and the Lord God shall give unto him the throne of his father David: 33 And he shall reign over the house of Jacob for ever; and of his kingdom there shall be no end. 34 Then said Mary unto the angel, How shall this be, seeing I know not a man? 35 And the angel answered and said unto her, The Holy Ghost shall come upon thee, and the power of the Highest shall overshadow thee: therefore also that holy thing which shall be born of thee shall be called the Son of God. 36 And, behold, thy cousin Elisabeth, she hath also conceived a son in her old age: and this is the sixth month with her, who was called barren. 37 For with God nothing shall be impossible. 38 And Mary said, Behold the handmaid of the Lord; be it unto me according to thy word. And the angel departed from her.

The story of Mary and Joseph begins in the region of Galilee in the tiny town of Nazareth, where Jesus grew up. In Elisabeth's sixth month, God sent Gabriel to Mary to announce she would miraculously bear a child who would be Israel's Messiah. Luke calls Nazareth a *polis* (**PA-lis**), which is translated "city," but it was a small "town" (NIV) or "village." Its unimportant size contrasts with Jerusalem, where Gabriel's previous appearance to Zacharias had taken place at the temple (**verse 19**). Galilee bordered Gentile nations; therefore, it was sometimes called Galilee of the Gentiles. The entire nation was under subjugation to the mighty Roman empire. Nazareth, was a despised city, considered inferior by the rest of Israel (**John 1:46**). The city and its citizens were disparaged and were belittled and the object of deep prejudice both by Jews and Romans.

God sent a message to a virgin (Gk. *parthenos*, **par THE-nos**) in Nazareth (Mary) and to a priest in Jerusalem (Zacharias). In the Greek translation of the Old Testament (commonly referred to as the Septuagint or LXX), *parthenos* means "girl," with chastity implied. Stress on chastity or virginity occurs in **Leviticus 21:13–14; Deuteronomy 22:23, 28;** and **2 Samuel 13:2**. When used with place names, it referred to non-pollution with idolatry. When used with the description of Mary, it meant she had not had sexual relations. Mary's question in **verse 34**, and the reference in **verse 27** to her being "espoused" or pledged to be married, make this clear. Since betrothal often took place soon after puberty, Mary may have been in the early part of her teenage years.

Betrothal was like an "engagement," but legally binding; to break it off was considered "divorce." According to Jewish custom and tradition, only divorce or death could sever betrothal; and in death, the unmarried girl would be a widow. Mary had already committed to marry Joseph, but she had not had sexual relations with him. In the betrothal period, sexual contact was considered adultery and resulted in stoning.

The phrase "house of David" explains the child would be born in David's line. David was Israel's greatest king, and God promised David that his kingdom would be everlasting (**2 Samuel 7:16**). The everlasting kingdom of David is fulfilled in Jesus. The angel greeted Mary and proclaimed she was highly favored, "having been much graced (by God)." "Highly favoured" translates the Greek word *kecharitomene* (**ke-khar-ee-TO-me-ne**), the same root as the words for "greetings" (*chaire*, **KHA-ee-reh**), and "grace of favour" (*charin*, **KHAR-een, verse 30**). Mary is "highly favoured" because she is the recipient of God's grace. But Mary was *greatly* troubled by the words of the angel. The Greek word *diatarasso* (**dee-at-ar-AS-so**) means to be confused or greatly perplexed. In contrast to Zacharias, who doubted the angel's words and required some sign before he could believe, Mary was perplexed but did not express doubt. Her terror at the sudden appearance of the angel—who probably appeared to her as a young man in strange, dazzling white garments—was not unfounded. Her perplexity was natural considering the sudden, unexpected appearance of an angel and the weight of the message the angel conveyed. She did not understand how God could so greatly favor a person like herself. Mary probably never dreamed she was anyone special. How could she, so ordinary and humble, do anything special for God? That is the essence of grace. What a striking example Mary was! Mary's favor was only by the grace of God. God reversed human expectations in Mary's situation, for He was willing to use the lowest in that time to be the bearer of a king. Today God continues to use the poor, the powerless, the helpless, and the weak (**2 Corinthians 12:9**).

The mighty work God foretold He would do through John the Baptist's ministry would be surpassed by an even greater work through His Son's ministry. Whereas John would be "great in the sight of the Lord" (**1:15**), Jesus would be great without qualification (**verse 32**) and would be "called the Son of God" (**verse 35**). An even more important tie between the accounts is that the whole significance of John's ministry, as pointed out in **verse 17**, is found in his preparation for the One coming after him who was more powerful than he (**3:16**).

Mary's question, "How shall this be?" was probably due to being puzzled rather than a question that arose from doubt or distrust. She was not asking for some sign or proof as Zacharias did (**1:18**). There is a world of difference between her request and that of Zacharias. Hers stemmed from her faith; the question of Zacharias stemmed from his lack of faith.

To ease any lingering apprehensions that Mary might have had, the angel informed her of another seemingly impossible situation: Elisabeth's pregnancy in her old age. Elisabeth was in her sixth month of pregnancy, again bearing testimony to the fact that nothing is impossible with God.

Mary's response to the angel was that she was only a servant of the Lord, which reveals her humility and further strengthens the reason why she had been chosen to bear the Messiah of Israel. Mary was a servant of God and would follow the words of God. No one could have asked for, or given, any better response. What a marvelous testimony to the magnificence of Mary! Her attitude of servanthood recalls that of Hannah in **1 Samuel 1:11**, where the LXX also has *doule* (**DOO-lay**), meaning "servant." Her servanthood consisted of a submission to God that characterized genuine believers in scripture and should characterize believers today (cf. **Luke 1:48**).

How do we respond to the words of God even when they seem impossible? Do we accept them with faith, remembering that we are humble servants of God? Or do we reject the words of God as impossible? Mary's trusting submission is a worthy example for believers today.

SEARCH THE SCRIPTURES

QUESTIONS

1. Jesus' earthly father Joseph's bloodline was of the _____?

2. Who was highly favored by the Lord?

II. MARY VISITS HER COUSIN (Luke 1:39–40)

It should be noted that Mary knew about Elisabeth's miraculous conception, but Elisabeth did not know about Mary's conception. This provides an important context for understanding Elisabeth's prophetic pronouncements that follow.

III. MARY VISITED ELISABETH (verses 39–40)

39 And Mary arose in those days, and went into the hill country with haste, into a city of Judah; 40 And entered into the house of Zacharias, and saluted Elisabeth.

After the departure of the angel, Mary paid a memorable visit to Elisabeth. She probably went so she and Elisabeth could encourage and share with each other. They both had similar situations. God had acted upon both their bodies, performing a miracle for both. Mary in particular could be encouraged, for Elisabeth was already six months pregnant, visible evidence that God had already acted upon her miraculously. When she arrived, Elisabeth greeted Mary with a prophecy—already knowing of Mary's pregnancy: "The babe leaped in her womb; and Elisabeth was filled with the Holy Ghost" **(1:41)**. This would have been a great encouragement to Mary.

BIBLE APPLICATION

AIM: Students will learn to not conform to this world but take a stand for righteousness.

Today, many people have babies together without being married. We celebrate the birth of children with parents as though we are following the way of the Lord. How often do we stop to consider the guidelines God has set for us? Fornication is a sin! We should marry before having sex. This is God's way. Let us not conform to this world. Let us take a stand for righteousness' sake. In addition, grandparents and church leaders should pray with unmarried couples with a child to consider marriage.

STUDENTS' RESPONSES

AIM: Students will live in a way that's pleasing to God.

God has given us guidelines to follow to give an accurate representation of Him. We should be mindful to live in such a way that Jesus' light in us is most dominant in any circumstance. Will your excitement for what the Lord has done be seen by others in the way you live?

PRAYER

Lord, we thank you for the coming of your Son Jesus. Lord, we thank you that He came to identify with our pain and suffering. We ask that you open our eyes to see how great He is and the blessing that comes from just knowing Him. We pray that you get all the worship and honor this holiday season. In Jesus' name, we pray. Amen.

DIG A LITTLE DEEPER

Mary was probably the most unexpectant person in the world. Given her status in society, she never thought she would be "highly favored" by anyone and most especially by God. After hearing the message of her selection and the pregnancy of her elder cousin, she had a choice: Stay or Go. Mary demonstrates great faith when she goes to visit her pregnant cousin Elizabeth. Mary could have hidden and waited to see if she was going to be pregnant. Like many of us, God has spoken but we are unable to fully accept the promise. What are some reasons Mary went to see Elizabeth? First Mary heard the Word of God about the prophecies concerning the Messiah. The Bible says that faith comes by hearing and hearing the Word of God (Romans 10:17 KJV). When the Angel spoke, it activated the Word planted in her heart. Second, she went to visit Elizabeth believing her cousin would be pregnant. Elizabeth had borne the shame of barrenness and pregnancy was almost unbelievable at her age. The Bible defines faith as the substance of things hoped for and evidence of things not seen (Hebrews 11:1KJV). I'm sure Mary was rehearsing the angelic proclamation and praising God for her cousin's miracle with every step she took toward Judea. Mary teaches us that faith requires action even for the impossible. Believe God. Hear His Word. Move Forward in Faith. Expect the Great.

HOW TO SAY IT

Gabriel. GAY-bree-elle.
Zacharias. za-kah-RAY-ahs.

PREPARE FOR NEXT SUNDAY

Read Luke 1:46–56 and study

"Mary's Praise Song."

Sources:
Hughes, R. Kent. *Luke (Volume One): That You May Know the Truth. Preaching the Word.* Wheaton, IL: Crossway, 1998.
Keener, Craig S. *The IVP Bible Background Commentary: New Testament.* Downers Grove, IL: IVP Academic, 1994.
Unger, Merrill F., R. K. Harrison, Howard Vos, and Cyril Barber. *The New Unger's Bible Dictionary.*
Chicago: Moody Publishers, 1988.
Preaching. Psalms. Louisville: John Knox Press, 1994. 331–337.
Mullins, Nicole C. "My Redeemer Lives." http://www.lyricsmode.com/lyrics/n/nicole_c_mullins/my_redeemer_lives.html (accessed December 19, 2012)

COMMENTS / NOTES:

DAILY HOME BIBLE READINGS

MONDAY
A Covenant with David
(Psalm 89:1 – 7)

TUESDAY
God's Faithfulness and Steadfast Love
(Psalm 89:19–24)

WEDNESDAY
The Highest of Earthly Kings
(Psalm 89:26–34)

THURSDAY
A Promise for a Distant Future
(2 Samuel 7: 18 – 29)

FRIDAY
A Child Name Immanuel
Isaiah (7:10 – 15)

SATURDAY
Elisabeth's Blessing
(Luke 1:41 – 45)

SUNDAY
The Announcement to Mary
(Luke 1:26 – 40)

MARY'S PRAISE SONG

BIBLE BASIS: LUKE 1:46–56

BIBLE TRUTH: God invites us to have real faith in Him.

MEMORY VERSE: "And my spirit hath rejoiced in God my Saviour" (Luke 1:47, KJV).

LESSON AIM: By the end of the lesson, we will: EXPLORE themes of justice in Mary's song of praise; APPRECIATE the deepest meanings of praise in response to God; and DEVELOP new ways of praising God.

BACKGROUND SCRIPTURES: Psalm 111 — Read and incorporate the insights gained from the Background Scriptures into your study of the lesson.

LESSON SCRIPTURE

LUKE 1:46–56, KJV

46 And Mary said, My soul doth magnify the Lord,

47 And my spirit hath rejoiced in God my Saviour.

48 For he hath regarded the low estate of his handmaiden: for, behold, from henceforth all generations shall call me blessed.

49 For he that is mighty hath done to me great things; and holy is his name.

50 And his mercy is on them that fear him from generation to generation.

51 He hath shewed strength with his arm; he hath scattered the proud in the imagination of their hearts.

52 He hath put down the mighty from their seats, and exalted them of low degree.

53 He hath filled the hungry with good things; and the rich he hath sent empty away.

54 He hath helped his servant Israel, in remembrance of his mercy;

55 As he spake to our fathers, to Abraham, and to his seed for ever.

56 And Mary abode with her about three months, and returned to her own house.

BIBLICAL DEFINITIONS

A. Blessed (Luke 1:48) *makaridzo* (Gk.)—To pronounce as fortunate or happy.
B. Mercy (v. 50) *elehos* (Gk.)—Divine or human compassion, tender mercy.

LIFE NEED FOR TODAY'S LESSON

AIM: Students will develop the practice of praise.

INTRODUCTION

Mary's Journey

Mary immediately decided to visit her aged, barren relative Elisabeth, who, as Gabriel had revealed, was pregnant and six months along (**1:36**). Her pregnancy was miraculous, but different from the miracle occurring within Mary. Barren

Elisabeth was not a virgin, and Zacharias was the natural father of her child. A surge of joy swept through Mary as she heard the shocking good news about the miracle in Elisabeth's womb, for it bore parallel testimony to God's power.

Luke reports Mary's response: "At that time Mary got ready and hurried to a town in the hill country of Judea" (**verse 39, NIV**). Mary made hasty arrangements with her parents and rushed 80 to 100 miles south to the countryside of Judea, a three- or four-day journey. Her haste indicates eagerness. She could not wait to get there. As she hurried, she thought long and deep of their crossed destinies, as she and Elisabeth were both in miraculous pregnancies.

BIBLE LEARNING

AIM: Students will get a clear understanding of who Jesus Christ is and His transforming power for all.

I. GOD IS WORTHY (Luke 1:46–50)

Mary experienced a wonderful visit with her cousin Elisabeth. So great, that upon Mary's arrival, the baby leaped in Elisabeth's womb. Elisabeth then praised God for what He was doing in having Mary visit her (**Luke 1:42–45**).

In response to Elisabeth's words, Mary recited a song that praised God's favor on her and her people. God alone was the center of her praise. Her song, the *Magnificat, consists* almost entirely of Old Testament allusions and quotations. In fact, the *Magnificat* closely resembles the song of Hannah in **1 Samuel**

2:1–10. Both open in similar exaltation of the Lord. Luke's Gospel is full of lowly people; from the shepherds that find themselves stable side for his birth to the inclusion of women and children. His account encourages us that God is concerned about the lowly. Mary says that God has regarded her lowly estate and closes her song with the soon-to-be consummated reality of God exalting the lowly and bringing low the strong and proud.

Mary saw herself as part of the godly remnant that had served Yahweh. She knew she had been chosen by God and privileged with carrying the Savior of the world. She called God "my Saviour," showing an intimate acquaintance with Him. She spoke of His faithfulness (**verse 48**), power (**verse 49**), holiness (**verse 49**), and mercy (**verse 50**).

God is the Subject of Her Song, Her Savior is Worthy (verses 46–50)
46 And Mary said, My soul doth magnify the Lord, 47 And my spirit hath rejoiced in God my Saviour. 48 For he hath regarded the low estate of his handmaiden: for, behold, from henceforth all generations shall call me blessed. 49 For he that is mighty hath done to me great things; and holy is his name. 50 And his mercy is on them that fear him from generation to generation.

Mary responded to Elisabeth's Spirit-inspired utterances in a song. The word "magnify" (Gk. *megalynei*, **meg-al-OO-ne-i**) means "to enlarge." It attributes greatness to God. To magnify means to make something appear larger than what it already is in order to have a better and proper perception. Think of a magnifying glass that a child uses to see an ant. The ant is small, but when the child looks through the glass, the ant seems large. God cannot appear larger because He is already bigger than we could ever imagine. Magnifying demands that we enlarge our *picture* of God. We often have a picture of God that is too small and contrived, so we need to magnify Him so we can have a better and bigger picture of Him.

The song is an expression of praise for what God had done to Mary. It opens with the declaration of her intention to magnify God in song (**verse 46**), which parallels the affirmation that she had found joy in God who enabled her in a miraculous way to become pregnant with the child of messianic hopes, had now intervened as Savior (**verse 47**). This happy state existed because God had regard for the afflicted state of His servant (**verse 48**). It was not that Mary had some personal and individual affliction; her affliction was that of God's people awaiting His saving intervention on their behalf. Hannah's affliction had been childlessness (**1 Samuel 1:11**); for God's people it may be spoken of as the lack of that child who was to be the messianic deliverer (**Isaiah 9:6**). The Messiah is a symbol of liberation, freedom, and salvation to the Israelites.

Although it has been noted the song has some similarities to Hannah's song in **1 Samuel 2:1–10**, it is equally noted that there is a difference between the two songs. Hannah proclaimed

triumph over her enemies, Mary proclaimed God and His glorious mercy to humanity. She proclaimed the salvation of God, salvation wrought through the promised Messiah, her Savior. Unlike many modern songs, Mary's song was not self-centered; she was not praising herself; God was the subject of her song, her praise, and rejoicing.

The greatness of the work of God is that it is a universal blessing to all. Jesus came so all people would be blessed. God blesses all because He is mighty and holy. He did a mighty work in the life of Mary that affected all people everywhere for all time. The King has come and will bring salvation.

Mary proclaimed God's power. She was in awe of "he that is mighty," the One whose great power had touched her life. The word "mighty" (*megala*, **meg AL-a**) recalls "magnify" (*megalynei*, **meg-al-OO-ne i**) in **verse 46**. Mary proclaimed God's holiness: "holy is his name"; God must be set apart as different from all others. His very nature, His very being, is different. God is both pure being and pure in being, perfect being and perfect in being, holy in name and holy in being. God's holiness has overtones of power and may be defined as His transcendent mightiness. **Verse 50** echoes **Psalm 103:17**, affirming what God was accomplishing in Mary: This act of God's mercy is for generation upon generation of those who fear Him. God's mercy is His active faithfulness to His covenant with Israel.

Mary proclaimed God's mercy with two thoughts in mind—what God had done in her life and what God had done in history. God has done mighty works throughout history, and God continues to do mighty works even into our own time. He has shown His mighty power, and God will take Israel by the hand and lead them to salvation.

SEARCH THE SCRIPTURES QUESTIONS

1. Mary speaks of Jesus' _____, _____, _____, and _____.

2. Who said the following words and are they true or false, "All generations shall call me blessed"?

II. GOD IS MIGHTY (Luke 1:51–56)

D.L. Moody has said, "Christ sends none away empty but those who are full of themselves." Who would that include? Mary gives us an idea in her song: the proud, the rich, self-sufficient, and rulers, all who demonstrate some level of behavior that is not God-honoring. That's the message here. As Christians, we need to constantly evaluate our lives to ensure we are not full of pride. We should never reach a point where our self-sufficiency removes the necessity of God in our daily lives, for He is our source. Finally, should we be blessed to have a leadership role, we should do so in humility, knowing we are under the authority of God. Our text closes recalling God's faithfulness to the Children of Israel. God had promised to be faithful to His people Israel forever because of the eternal covenant He had made by oath with their forefathers

(e.g., **Deuteronomy 7:7–8**).

God Helped His People (verses 51–56)

51 He hath shewed strength with his arm; he hath scattered the proud in the imagination of their hearts. 52 He hath put down the mighty from their seats, and exalted them of low degree. 53 He hath filled the hungry with good things; and the rich he hath sent empty away. 54 He hath helped his servant Israel, in remembrance of his mercy; 55 As he spake to our fathers, to Abraham, and to his seed forever. 56 And Mary abode with her about three months and returned to her own house.

Mary proceeded from adoration to celebration. She saw into the future and proclaimed what the Messiah's coming would accomplish. She prophetically spoke as though the future had become the past, as though the child yet to be born had already lived and done His mighty work in the world. She recognized the strength of God's "arm" which, in old days, had wrought mighty things for Israel. Mary showed that God will reverse the order of things on earth.

At the end of time, the Lord will scatter the proud "in the imagination of their hearts." Although the Greek word *dianoia* (**dee-AN-oy-ah**), translated for "imagination," may ordinarily refer to a mode of thinking, its combination with *kardias* (**kar DEE-as**), "heart," connotes arrogance or pride in human thoughts, intents, or attitudes. The Lord will dethrone the mighty and exalt the humble. The mighty are those who sit in positions of power, authority and influence over others. Those rich only in the things of this world will be stripped of all their earthly goods and sent away empty. Those who have nothing of this world, but who put their trust in God, will receive all the good things that God will provide.

BIBLE APPLICATION

AIM: Students will understand they can trust God for all of His promises.

It is so much easier to follow than to lead. We have a tendency to look around and see what the rest of the world is doing and then follow suit. It is time for God's people to appropriately represent Him in the way we live. Our reflection of Christ should show up in the way we obey our God and in the way, we encourage one another to do the same.

STUDENTS' RESPONSES

AIM: Students will put the principles of Christ to use in their daily walk.

When we study God's Word, we are reminded of His promises. Our faith is shown in the way we obey God. Let's take a closer look at how we express praise to God in our actions. Mary's obedience gave praise to God! In the upcoming week, begin to follow Mary's lead and praise God in the way you obey Him.

PRAYER

Father, we worship and praise you for the gift that you have given us in your Son Jesus Christ. We thank you for all the blessings we receive because of His finished work on the cross. Lord, we ask that you help us to follow in the footsteps of Jesus and that you use us to show the world that you are still active today. In Jesus' name, we pray. Amen.

DIG A LITTLE DEEPER

Mary expressed her faith by believing the prophecy received from God and traveling to see her cousin Elizabeth. Mary's arrival causes the promise in Elizabeth to activate. The Holy Spirit in response to faith in the Word of God results in a joyful response from Elizabeth, John, and Mary. Elizabeth's song of praise was for the mother of her promised Messiah. The Holy Spirit prophesied through Elizabeth to confirm the prophecy received by Mary. John, who was alive in the womb, responded in praise at the arrival of his Messiah. As Mary realizes the fulfillment of prophecy, the Word of God received, it brought forth a joyful response in her. Her obedience to the Word of God about the promise of Messiah resulted in words of affirmation about who she was in God's eyes. Mary magnified the Lord because the Lord regarded someone of her lowly status. She continues her magnification of our Lord because the promise of the Messiah would bless everybody in similar lowly status. Whether that status is societal or spiritual, Messiah was coming for everybody. Her joyful response was ultimately about the blessing to all of Israel who God promised to redeem as His people. Our praise results from obedience to the Word of God. The Word responds to our faith and fills us with the Holy Spirit which erupts in a joyful response.

As Nehemiah 8:10 states, the joy of the Lord is my strength. Mary's song of praise equipped her with he strength to carry forth the promise which would bless us today. Our praise should result not only in physical exercise but spiritual empowerment that blesses everyone around us

HOW TO SAY IT

Magnificat. mag-**NI**-fi-kat.

Messiah. mes-**EYE**-ah.

PREPARE FOR NEXT SUNDAY

Read **Luke 1:57–58, 67–79** and study "Zacharias Prophesies About His Son John."

Sources:
Cambridge Advanced Learner's Dictionary & Thesaurus.
Cambridge Dictionaries Online. http://dictionary.cambridge.org/dictionary/british/ (accessed July 25, 2012).
Keener, Craly S. The IVP Bible Background Commentary: New Testament. Downers Grove, IL: IVP Academic, 1994

COMMENTS / NOTES:

_____
_____
_____
_____
_____
_____
_____
_____
_____

DAILY HOME BIBLE READINGS

MONDAY
My Heart Exults in the Lord
(1 Samuel 2:1–10)

TUESDAY
Oh, Magnify the Lord with Me
(Psalm 34:1–8)

WEDNESDAY
Give Thanks to the Lord
(Psalm 100)

THURSDAY
Bless the Compassionate Lord
(Psalm 103:13–22)

FRIDAY
Praise the Gracious and Merciful Lord
(Psalm 111)

SATURDAY
The Lord Reigns for All
Generations (Psalm 146)

SUNDAY
God Has Done Great Things
(Luke 1:46–56)

ZACHARIAS' PROPHESIES ABOUT JOHN

BIBLE BASIS: LUKE 1:57–38, 67–79

BIBLE TRUTH: God rewards faith and punishes unbelief.

MEMORY VERSE: "And thou, child, shalt be called the prophet of the Highest: for thou shalt go before the face of the Lord to prepare his ways; To give knowledge of salvation unto his people by the remission of their sins" (Luke 1:76–77, KJV).

LESSON AIM: By the end of the lesson, we will: REVIEW the story of Zacharias' prophecy concerning his son, John the Baptist; GAIN an appreciation for prophecy and REFLECT on expectations we have for the next generation; and address the justice modeled in Zacharias' prophecy.

BACKGROUND SCRIPTURES: Luke 1:59-66, 67-69 — Read and incorporate the insights gained from the Background Scriptures into your study of the lesson.

LESSON SCRIPTURE

LUKE 1:57–58, 67–79, KJV

57 Now Elisabeth's full time came that she should be delivered; and she brought forth a son.

58 And her neighbours and her cousins heard how the Lord had shewed great mercy upon her; and they rejoiced with her.

67 And his father Zacharias was filled with the Holy Ghost, and prophesied, saying,

68 Blessed be the Lord God of Israel; for he hath visited and redeemed his people,

69 And hath raised up an horn of salvation for us in the house of his servant David;

70 As he spake by the mouth of his holy prophets, which have been since the world began:

71 That we should be saved from our enemies, and from the hand of all that hate us;

72 To perform the mercy promised to our fathers, and to remember his holy covenant;

73 The oath which he sware to our father Abraham,

74 That he would grant unto us, that we being delivered out of the hand of our enemies might serve him without fear,

75 In holiness and righteousness before him, all the days of our life.

76 And thou, child, shalt be called the prophet of the Highest: for thou shalt go before the face of the Lord to prepare his ways;

77 To give knowledge of salvation unto his people by the remission of their sins,

78 Through the tender mercy of our God; whereby the dayspring from on high hath visited us,

79 To give light to them that sit in darkness and in the shadow of death, to guide our feet into the way of peace.

BIBLICAL DEFINITIONS

A. Prophesy (Luke 1:67) *propheteuo* (Gk.)—To speak forth by divine inspiration, to predict; sometimes with the idea of foretelling future events pertaining especially to the kingdom of God.

B. Dayspring (v. 78) *anatole* (Gk.)—A rising of the sun and stars; the dawn.

LIFE NEED FOR TODAY'S LESSON

AIM: Students will learn that nothing is impossible with God.

INTRODUCTION

Birth Announcements

Chapter 1 begins with Luke informing readers his only purpose in writing this book was to make a truthful record of Jesus' birth. He recounted how Zacharias was working in the temple when the angel Gabriel announced Elisabeth would give birth to a son. Zacharias questioned Gabriel's words, his voice was taken away, and he couldn't speak until his son was born. Elisabeth hid herself for five months. In her sixth month, Luke focused on Mary, Elisabeth's cousin. Mary also received a surprise visit from Gabriel with the same announcement—she, too, would bear a son. But her pregnancy would not result from relations with a man but through the overshadowing of the Holy Spirit. Unlike Zacharias, Mary believed Gabriel; hurried to visit Elisabeth, then stayed three months.

BIBLE LEARNING

AIM: Students will learn from biblical history the relationship of prophecy and faith.

I. REJOICING WITH ELISABETH (LUKE 1:57–58).

When Elisabeth's female friends, neighbors, and relatives were becoming menopausal and grandmothers, Elisabeth became pregnant. Due to age, she had to take care of her body, save her strength, and preserve her health to carry a baby full term. There was exceeding joy in her heart and soul when she delivered a healthy baby boy, John. God had finally shown great mercy upon her. She and her circle of family and friends celebrated and praised the birth of her miracle baby.

Praises for Elisabeth (verses 57–58)

57 Now Elisabeth's full time came that she should be delivered; and she brought forth a son. 58 And her neighbours and her cousins heard how the Lord had shewed great mercy upon her; and they rejoiced with her.

Elisabeth was the second cousin of Mary, the mother of Jesus. Both of their babies had divine origins, for the angel Gabriel stood before Zacharias in the temple just as he stood before Mary. Zacharias and Elisabeth differed from Mary for they were old so pregnancy seemed like a lost cause. The promise did come true, and even in the womb their baby was already filled with the Holy Ghost and leaped with joy in response to hearing the voice of Mary when she visited (**Luke 1:15, 44**). For three months, Mary and Elisabeth spent time together, probably preparing the home for the baby. Just after Mary left, Elisabeth gave birth to a baby boy.

The Jewish custom for welcoming babies was music, food, and celebration. Family and neighbors would gather for a party and wait to hear if a boy or girl was born, anxiously hoping for a boy, maybe the Messiah. Boys took on greater significance than girls. One theologian said if a boy was born, musicians would start playing, people would dance and party. If a girl was born, musicians would leave, and there would be no great celebration. This may be why the word "mercy" (Gk. *eleos*, **eh-LEE-ose**) is used because it indicates a unique kindness or good will toward someone who is afflicted.

SEARCH THE SCRIPTURES

QUESTION

Elisabeth's neighbors and cousins rejoiced with her because the Lord had shown her what?

II. PRAISES FOR GOD
(Luke 1:67–75)

Zacharias endured more than 270 days of scribbling requests, grunting to emphasize what he used to easily say, and gesturing with his hands. He made it through the delivery of his son, but when Zacharias opened his mouth, he did not praise himself, his wife, or his son. He blessed Jesus, the child still to be born.

Promises for Jesus (verses 67–75)

67 And his father Zacharias was filled with the Holy Ghost, and prophesied, saying: 68 Blessed be the Lord God of Israel; for he hath visited and redeemed his people. 69 And hath raised up an horn of salvation for us in the house of his servant David. 70 As he spake by the mouth of his holy prophets, which have been since the world began. 71 That we should be saved from our enemies, and from the hand of all that hate us. 72 To perform the mercy promised to our fathers, and to remember his holy covenant. 73 The oath which he sware to our father Abraham. 74 That he would grant unto us, that we being delivered out of the hand of our enemies might serve him with out fear. 75 In holiness and righteousness before him, all the days of our life.

Being filled with the Holy Ghost (Gk. *pneuma*, **NOO-ma**) during this time was a rare gift. Zacharias, a priest from the line of Aaron, was the first person God spoke to through an angel about his baby's birth. He'd been divinely struck mute since this happened due to his unbelief. Now that the events had come to pass, God blessed Zacharias with Himself and the return of his voice. Biblical prophecies often begin with praises of who God is and then move into a personal application or promise. Zacharias' praise, the *Benedictus*, is a Latin term to describe his praise to God. Even though he could have been angry at God for the punishment of not being able to speak for nine months, he instead celebrated who the Lord is and what He was about to do. This song can be divided into two sections, including an initial burst of thanksgiving that then leads into an address from Zacharias to his son. It reveals his personal thrill at seeing his household take part in the great purpose of God to save all people.

Jews commonly saw a horn as a symbol of strength, so a "horn of salvation" means a mighty Savior. God is described this way in **Psalm 18**, so by sharing similar sentiments here, Zacharias provides another link to the Trinity through the birth of Jesus. People viewed the reign of David as a time when Israel held power to defend itself against its enemies. The coming Messiah would again put the Jews in a place of prominence, but in a divine, spiritual sense versus merely a political one.

This is the meaning behind what true salvation (Gk. *soteria*, **sow-TAY-ree-ah**) is. Deliverance is more than protection from physical oppression; it also affects internal and ethical issues like humanity's sin. The Messiah would present both to Christians, but in stages: personal transformation that would lead to an eternal dwelling with God when the kingdom of God arrives in fullness.

Zacharias affirmed that all that was taking place was in accordance with God's promises to His people in the past. In each verse that follows, Zacharias tracked a chronology of different core events Jews experienced in waiting for their Messiah. Zacharias simultaneously fulfilled his roles as a priest and prophet by pouring out worship toward the Lord and instructing others to remember their people's story.

By sending someone like John the Baptist who would prepare the way for the Messiah, God declared t h a t the p e o p l e had not been forgotten. They endured the scorn of surrounding nations and their Roman oppressors but were never without the promise that God would one day save them. God visited His people when they were captive in Egypt (**Exodus 3:16, 4:31**) and then continued to send them numerous prophets throughout succeeding generations, it was time for the Lord to supernaturally save His people from all that stood against them. It began with John, who would remind them of their sin so that Christ alone would be shown to be the Savior.

A covenant (Gk. *diatheke*, **dee-ah-tha-KAH**) is a unique arrangement that's valid between a superior party and a lesser party. The one with more power or authority would initiate the arrangement, finalize the terms, and then validate things through a symbolic sacrifice. God always played the stronger role, and Israel the yielding role.

III. PROMISES FOR THE CHILD (Luke 1:76–79)

Zacharias had endured years of his wife's barrenness and months of silence, so he wondered what kind of child John would be. Knowing he had not suffered in vain, Zacharias declared an affirmation of Gabriel's earlier message "And thou, child, shalt be called the prophet of the Highest." Zacharias needed only to look to Hebrew Scripture for evidence of John's future: John would be the servant who would prepare the way of the Lord (**Isaiah 40:3**). John would be the prophet to call the people of Israel to repentance. Even with his limited understanding of the entire story, Zacharias spoke life over his son, proclaiming his purpose and establishing him as the forerunner for Christ.

Prophecies for John (verses 76–79)
76 And thou, child, shalt be called the prophet of the Highest: for thou shalt go before the face of the Lord to prepare his ways. 77 To give knowledge of salvation unto his people by the remission of their sins, 78 Through the tender mercy of our

God; whereby the dayspring from on high hath visited us. 79 To give light to them that sit in darkness and in the shadow of death, to guide our feet into the way of peace.

Isaiah 40:3 speaks about the forerunner of the Messiah, and John himself would later own this truth and claim it publicly (**John 1:23**). Zacharias knew this pattern as a priest, for as Aaron was Moses' mouthpiece (**Exodus 7:1**), so would John be a messenger to prepare people for salvation and the kingdom of heaven. He would preach repentance by calling people to open their hearts to the Lord.

Psalm 56:13 states, "For thou hast delivered my soul from death: wilt not thou deliver my feet from falling, that I may walk before God in the light of the living?" Zacharias said the Messiah would not just reveal sins but actually purify people of their sins. This freedom is more than being delivered out of the hands of enemies—it involves forgiveness of what we've done wrong and the sin nature that corrupts us, and then it enables us to have a relationship with God.

The ability to even know that John would be a prophet who would prepare the way for the Messiah was a sign that Zacharias was speaking under divine guidance, knowing things that only the Holy Ghost could have revealed to him. By speaking even now about Jesus, whom he didn't know, Zacharias revealed his relationship to the God he did know. There is also a backdrop for this statement from Isaiah 60:1–2 that says, "Arise, shine; for thy light is come, and the glory of the LORD is risen upon thee. For, behold, the darkness shall cover the earth, and gross darkness the people: but the LORD shall arise upon thee, and his glory shall be seen upon thee."

Jesus Christ is more than the giver of salvation, and John the Baptist was more than His forerunner. Each offered a light in the darkness that humanity needed to find the way back to a peace that only the Lord can provide. Christ is the morning Light and rising Sun (**Malachi 4:2**). Through John the Baptist, this light began to break into the darkness of sin, increasing until the Messiah shone it in perfect brilliance through His character, teachings, and mission.

SEARCH THE SCRIPTURES

QUESTION

What was John's role in relationship to Christ?

BIBLE APPLICATION

AIM: Students will understand that God is displeased with unbelief as well as belief.

We live in a society that prides itself upon its right to exercise freedom of speech. Though we can freely say whatever we think and feel, this lesson shows we ought to exercise our right to remain silent. What if we were arrested every time we spoke against the Lord? Zacharias' ability to speak was taken away when he verbalized unbelief. Growing up, we are taught how and when to speak. Spiritual maturity is evidenced by those who know how and when *not* to speak.

STUDENTS' RESPONSES

AIM: Students will begin to use positive words instead of negative ones.

This week, challenge yourself to practice something you learned when you were a child—to only speak if you have something nice to say. Enjoy a week without complaining, cursing, or criticizing. It should be a week of positivity.

PRAYER

Father, we praise you because we know that nothing is impossible for you. You are the all-powerful God of the universe. We thank you that you chose to call us your people and we can call on you in prayer. Lord, we ask that you strengthen our hearts so we can walk by faith and believe you for the impossible things in our lives. In Jesus' name, we pray. Amen.

DIG A LITTLE DEEPER

Zacharias was the priest who was silenced because of his unbelief. The primary tool for a priest was his voice. It was his voice that was used to offer prayers for the people, to give praise to God, and to provide instruction to the people. For the entire pregnancy, Zecharias watched in silence as the miracle manifested because it would be at this point, his voice was to return according to Angel Gabriel. Once the child was born, he wrote down that his name was to be John and immediately his voice returned.

The Bible says John was filled with the Holy Spirit and began to prophesy. Zecharias became the first person to demonstrate the redemptive power of God. When we operate in faith and obedience, God will be with us and in us. Zechariah prophesied about the redemption that was to come to all the world. Zechariah shows us that God is mindful of us and loves us. The months of silence suffered by Zecharias mirrored the years of silence experienced by the world. Zecharia's restoration would be the example for all mankind that the Savior was coming to restore us to God and our purpose on earth.

HOW TO SAY IT

Zacharias. za-ka-**ri**-as.

Prophesied. **PRA**-fa-sid.

PREPARE FOR NEXT SUNDAY

Read **Luke 2:1–17** and study "The Messiah Arrives."

Sources:
Blue Letter Bible. BlueLetterBible.org. http://www.blueletterbible.org/commentaries/comm_view.cfm?AuthorID=1&contentID=7140&commInfo=25&topic=Luke&ar=Luk_1_57 (accessed August 28, 2012).
Smith, William. *Smith's Bible Dictionary*. Peabody, MA: Hendrickson Publishers, Inc., 2000. 137, 366–67, 539–41.
Word in Life Study Bible (NKJV). Nashville: Thomas Nelson Publishers, 1993. 167, 755.

COMMENTS / NOTES:

DAILY HOME BIBLE READINGS

MONDAY
What Will This Child Become?
(Luke 1:59–66)

TUESDAY
John's Call to Repentance
(Luke 3:1–6)

WEDNESDAY
What Then Should We Do?
(Luke 3:7–14)

THURSDAY
One More Powerful than John
(Luke 3:15–20)

FRIDAY
The Baptizer of Jesus
(Matthew 3:13–17)

SATURDAY
A Prophet and More
(Luke 7:18–27)

SUNDAY
A Prophet of the Most High
(Luke 1:57–58, 67–79)

THE MESSIAH ARRIVES

BIBLE BASIS: LUKE 2:1—17

BIBLE TRUTH: he Messiah was born.

MEMORY VERSE: "And she brought forth her firstborn son, and wrapped him in swaddling clothes, and laid him in a manger; because there was no room for them in the inn" (Luke 2:7, KJV).

LESSON AIM: By the end of the lesson, we will: REVIEW the story of Joseph and Mary's journey to Bethlehem and Jesus' birth; REFLECT on the meaning of the Messiah in contemporary times; and IDENTIFY the saving work of Jesus in the world today.

BACKGROUND SCRIPTURES: Galatians 4:1–7, Luke 1, Isaiah 7:14, John 1:11 — Read and incorporate the insights gained from the Background Scriptures into your study of the lesson.

LESSON SCRIPTURE

LUKE 2:1–17, KJV

1 And it came to pass in those days, that there went out a decree from Caesar Augustus that all the world should be taxed.

2 (And this taxing was first made when Cyrenius was governor of Syria.)

3 And all went to be taxed, every one into his own city.

4 And Joseph also went up from Galilee, out of the city of Nazareth, into Judaea, unto the city of David, which is called Bethlehem; (because he was of the house and lineage of David:)

5 To be taxed with Mary his espoused wife, being great with child.

6 And so it was, that, while they were there, the days were accomplished that she should be delivered.

7 And she brought forth her firstborn son, and wrapped him in swaddling clothes, and laid him in a manger; because there was no room for them in the inn.

8 And there were in the same country shepherds abiding in the field, keeping watch over their flock by night.

9 And, lo, the angel of the Lord came upon them, and the glory of the Lord shone round about them: and they were sore afraid.

10 And the angel said unto them, Fear not: for, behold, I bring you good tidings of great joy, which shall be to all people.

11 For unto you is born this day in the city of David a Saviour, which is Christ the Lord.

12 And this shall be a sign unto you; Ye shall find the babe wrapped in swaddling clothes, lying in a manger.

13 And suddenly there was with the angel a multitude of the heavenly host praising God, and saying,

14 Glory to God in the highest, and on earth peace, good will toward men.

15 And it came to pass, as the angels were gone away from them into heaven, the shepherds said one to another, Let us now go even unto Bethlehem, and see this thing which is come to pass, which the Lord hath made known unto us.

16 And they came with haste, and found Mary, and Joseph, and the babe lying in a manger.

17 And when they had seen it, they made known abroad the saying which was told them concerning this child.

BIBLICAL DEFINITIONS

A. Decree (Luke 2:1) *dogma* (Gk.)— Doctrine, ordinance. The rules and requirements of the Law of Moses, carrying a suggestion of severity and threatened judgment.
B. Espoused (v. 5) *mnesteuo* (Gk.)—To be promised in marriage; engaged.
C. Manger (v. 7) *phatne* (Gk.)—Stall, a compartment for one domestic animal in a barn or shed.

LIFE NEED FOR TODAY'S LESSON

AIM: Students will believe Jesus was born and God's promise was kept.

INTRODUCTION

The Census

Joseph and Mary were preparing for the arrival of their first born when Rome made a decree for a census. Although close to her due date, the couple made a 90-mile journey from Nazareth to Bethlehem. To fulfill God's promise, Jesus had to be born in Bethlehem, the City of David, where his parents had to pay hometown taxes.

BIBLE LEARNING

AIM: Students will learn that Jesus fulfilled all Scriptures concerning the coming Messiah.

I. PREPARING FOR THE BIRTH (Luke 2:1–6)

Joseph and Mary had probably prepared a place for the baby in their home, chosen His first outfit, and made sure they had a well-practiced first-century version of Lamaze breathing ready for Mary's labor and delivery. Then, Caesar issued a decree— every man had to go to his hometown to be taxed.

This taxing process was all part of God's plan because Bethlehem held a special place in scripture. It was King David's hometown and was where the expected Messiah was to be born (**Micah 5:1; cf. Matthew 2:1**). The tax wasn't necessarily a Caesar idea, but a God idea. It caused two people who lived in Nazareth to journey to Bethlehem in a prophecy-fulfilling moment in history.

Guess what happened when the couple got to Bethlehem? Mary's contractions began. With no rooms in the inns, the couple was forced to seek shelter in a barn. There in a stall, the first witnesses to the Messiah's birth were animals.

Going Back (verses 1–6)

1 And it came to pass in those days, that there went out a decree from Caesar Augustus that all the world should be taxed. 2 (And this taxing was first made when Cyrenius was governor of Syria.) 3 And all went to be taxed, every one into his own city. 4 And Joseph also went up from Galilee, out of the city of Nazareth, into Judaea, unto the city of David, which is called Bethlehem; (because he was of the house and lineage of David:) 5 To be taxed with Mary his espoused wife, being great with child. 6 And so it was, that, while they were there, the days were

accomplished that she should be delivered.

The phrase "those days" refers to an era of oppression under the Roman empire. Caesar Augustus was born Gaius Octavius, the grandnephew of Julius Caesar. Since Julius Caesar had legally adopted Octavius as his son, Octavius took the name "Caesar" from Julius, which later became a name almost equal to "emperor." The term "Augustus" in Latin means "worthy of reverence," showing how Romans used titles with overtones of pagan divinity. He reigned as emperor for 41 years from 27 B.C. to

A.D. 14, a time of political security and lavish building projects. Augustus restored 82 temples in Rome alone and became an object of worship in the state religion, although he emphasized a return to worship the old gods that had made Rome great.

Taxing the whole world took place regionally, and everyone in power tended to receive some form of a profit from it. The Greek verb used for this taxing is *apographa* (**a-po-gra-FA**) **meaning** to "enroll" or "register," like in an official listing of citizens. The census was called "taxing" because once everyone was accounted for, they could be more accurately taxed, plus Augustus wanted to know whether the population of his empire was growing for he was interested in all the nations Rome had absorbed. This "first" or "prior" census (taxing) was distinguished from the later one Luke mentions in **Acts 5:37**. Even people who lived far away from their home city had to return for the census.

The trip from Nazareth to Bethlehem was about 90 miles, going upward to an elevation of 2,300 feet above sea level. Joseph "went up" on a journey that

was a significant undertaking of days, travel and expense. Luke recorded the territories they crossed as a reference point so Jews would also recognize that Bethlehem was an area first mentioned in **Genesis 35:19**, then **48:7**, **Judges 12:8–10**, and **Ruth 1:1–19**. Bethlehem was a small, humble village, but Micah prophesied that the Messiah would be born there (**Micah 5:2**). He would be the "Son of David," and Bethlehem was where David had been born and raised (**1 Samuel 16:1**).

Joseph is mentioned as being a descendant of David, while nothing was said of Mary's genealogy. Mary was described as espoused or engaged to Joseph. This arrangement was legally established; therefore, to break it off would be considered divorce. **Matthew 1:24** clarifies Joseph took Mary as his wife before Jesus was born. Mary's controversial pregnancy would have left her under fire had she remained home while Joseph went to Bethlehem.

II. ANNOUNCING THE BIRTH (Luke 2:7–12)

While the Messiah and His parents slept, the shepherds were in a field keeping watch over their sheep. The evening started out as routine as any other and the shepherds brought the sheep back to the fold.

Coming Forth (verses 7–12)

7 And she brought forth her firstborn son, and wrapped him in swaddling clothes, and laid him in a manger; because there was no room for them in the inn. 8 And there were in the same country shepherds abiding in the field, keeping watch over their flock by night. 9 And, lo, the angel of the Lord came upon them, and the glory of the Lord shone round about

them: and they were sore afraid. 10 And the angel said unto them, Fear not: for, behold, I bring you good tidings of great joy, which shall be to all people. 11 For unto you is born this day in the city of David a Saviour, which is Christ the Lord. 12 And this shall be a sign unto you; Ye shall find the babe wrapped in swaddling clothes, lying in a manger.

Since the census affected all of Joseph's family, there were probably family members there taking part in a type of reunion. There is also no indication that Mary had any help in giving birth for she brought forth her own baby, wrapped Him in clothes, and placed Him in the manger.

Shepherds made little money and were on the low end of the social scale. Due to long periods of time out in the fields with sheep, they couldn't keep up with the ceremonial cleansing rituals that Orthodox Jewish leaders demanded so they often smelled bad. Although their profession was necessary and honored, shepherds were seen as second-class people.

God's glory appeared with this unnamed angel as a brilliant light, just as it had in other passages (**Isaiah 60:1; Ezekiel 1:28, 10:4; Matthew 17:5**). Like Zacharias and Mary, the shepherds were shocked when they saw the angel. Then, the angel told the shepherds the same thing said to others: "Fear not." Until you have a fear of God, you won't hear the invitation to no longer be afraid of Him.

The pronouncement of Jesus' birth was presented as a gift, not only to everyone but also to these particular people. Most groups of shepherds during that era would include a mixture of ages and backgrounds, from career shepherds to

those training. It may have also included girls who hadn't had a physical transition into womanhood, for once they did they would go home and serve alongside their mothers. This announcement to those on the margins of society is indicative of God's concern for all of us, including those most may ignore.

The angel promised a tangible sign to validate the claims, which follows a pattern throughout the Bible of how God promised something, pledged to do it within certain circumstances, and then offered visible proof that He would follow through.

The virgin birth itself was a sign (**Isaiah 7:14**), but in this instance the focus was on Jesus and not His mother. While she had used the common clothes and feeding trough to care for her baby, these natural elements would become supernatural markers for the shepherds.

SEARCH THE SCRIPTURES

QUESTION

Describe the setting and how the shepherds responded to the angel who shared with them the great news of Jesus' birth.

III. SHARING THE BIRTH
(Luke 2:13–17)

If the shepherds had any doubt about what they saw and heard was true, there next appeared a host of praising angels. Heaven was excited about this newborn Savior, and the least the shepherds could do was verify the sign they'd been given. They went quickly to Bethlehem.

Spreading Out (verses 13–17)

13 And suddenly there was with the angel a multitude of the heavenly

host praising God, and saying, 14 Glory to God in the highest, and on earth peace, good will toward men. 15 And it came to pass, as the angels were gone away from them into heaven, the shepherds said one to another, Let us now go even unto Bethlehem, and see this thing which is come to pass, which the Lord hath made known unto us. 16 And they came with haste, and found Mary, and Joseph, and the babe lying in a manger. 17 And when they had seen it, they made known abroad the saying which was told them concerning this child.

The angel was suddenly joined by a great multitude of angels. The Greek word for "host" is *stra tia,* which refers to an army, a band of soldiers, or a troop of angels. These weren't cute little angel cherubs with fat cheeks, but military-level angels. As heavenly soldiers, they understood the amazing event taking place at that moment on earth, so they proclaimed it.

The angels even went to invite others to respond. The phrase "Glory to God in the highest" means to force yourself to a new place of worship in response to who God is. It's as if heaven itself cracked open momentarily and the shadowy world had light and song.

The Bible contains the names of several people who we know very little. In contrast, these shepherds were among the first to see the face of Jesus, and they remain unnamed. These unnamed shepherds will forever have the honor of being the first ones outside of the holy family to hear of the birth of Jesus. God ordained it for them, which perhaps is how they mysteriously found Christ in the middle of the night during a busy census season. They found Him asleep in a manger, just as the angel had said.

SEARCH THE SCRIPTURES

QUESTION

What were the angels saying as they were praising God for the birth of the Messiah?

BIBLE APPLICATION

AIM: Students will understand that almost every God-given promise is surrounded by problems.

We live in a society where people think that God's promises are easy to obtain. They say, "What God has for me is for me," until they come upon hardship. Then they say, "I must've heard God wrong." Almost every God-given promise is shrouded by problems. The path from Egypt led straight to the Red Sea. The Promised Land had giants in it. Jesus' birth was redirected by a census that caused a series of unfortunate events. We must learn to persist and endure if we are ever going to be witnesses of the greater things of God.

STUDENTS' RESPONSES

AIM: Students will learn to trust God despite obstacles.

What promise has God made to you? Make a list of the obstacles you're enduring and remember Mary and Joseph. Know that each obstacle gets you closer to the promise. Praise God in advance for the birth of the promise He's entrusted to you.

PRAYER

Father, we thank you for bringing your Word to pass. You brought your Word to pass in sending your Son Jesus. We know that you can bring your Word to pass in our lives. We ask that you would have your way in our lives and we would obey your Word in everything that we do. In Jesus' name, we pray. Amen.

DIG A LITTLE DEEPER

Being a Shepherd was not a highly regarded job. The job negatively impacted relationships as it separated them from family, church, and community. The job was in a constant state of instability as it required them to move for food and shelter. A shepherd was exposed to danger continually such as thieves coming to steal the flock and wild animals coming to eat the flock. Unrealistic expectations only to survive on a meager income. It is in the midst of this situation that God chose to share his glorious announcement about the birth of his Son, Jesus, the savior of the world. The bright glorious burst of light that shined in the darkness of the shepherd's life is symbolic of Jesus' role. Jesus came to save the world from their wickedness and reconcile man back to a right relationship with God but he also came to bring hope to our real-life situations. While the shepherds found themselves back in the darkness, the message of hope inspired them to go and find the promised Messiah. This is the hope for the world today, despite your status in society and the state of your condition, Jesus can still be found. Believers have to shine the light like the angelic host and tell the message of Jesus.

HOW TO SAY IT

Bethlehem. **beth**-li-hem.

Nazareth. **na**-za-reth.

Cyrenius. **CY**-ren-ee-us.

PREPARE FOR NEXT SUNDAY

Read **Luke 2:25–38** and study "Jesus, Simeon & Anna."

Sources:
Faithhelper.com. "Is Bible God's Words?" http://www.faithhelper.com/ntrel3.htm (accessed September 11, 2012).
Potter, D. S. "Life, Death and Entertainment in the Roman Empire." UNRV History.
http://www.unrv.com/book-review/life-death entertainment.php (accessed September 12, 2012). Smith, William. *Smith's Bible Dictionary*. Peabody, MA:
Hendrickson Publishers, Inc., 2000. 137, 322–23, 386, 617–18.

COMMENTS / NOTES:

_____
_____
_____
_____

DAILY HOME BIBLE READINGS

MONDAY
A Child Dedicated to the Lord
(1 Samuel 1:21–28)

TUESDAY
Blessing the Children of Israel
(Numbers 6:22–27)

WEDNESDAY
Hope for the Coming One
(Isaiah 9:1–5)

THURSDAY
A Ruler from Bethlehem and Judah
(Micah 5:1–5)

FRIDAY
God's Blessings on David's Descendants
(Psalm 18:46–50)

SATURDAY
The Fullness of Time
(Galatians 4:1–7)

SUNDAY
The Birth of Jesus in Bethlehem
(Luke 2:1–17)

JESUS, SIMEON & ANNA

BIBLE BASIS: LUKE 2:25—38

BIBLE TRUTH: God always honors His promise to the faithful.

MEMORY VERSE: "For mine eyes have seen thy salvation, Which thou hast prepared before the face of all people" (Luke 2:30–31, KJV).

LESSON AIM: y the end of the lesson, we will: EXPLORE Jesus' presentation in the Temple; EXPRESS our feelings about the phrase "This child is set for the fall and rising again of many" (from Luke 2:34); and DECIDE how we might walk in holiness.

BACKGROUND SCRIPTURES: Isaiah 49:8–13, Exodus 13:12, Gen. 17:10-12 and Luke 2:1-24 — Read and incorporate the insights gained from the Background Scriptures into your study of the lesson.

LESSON SCRIPTURE

LUKE 2:25–38, KJV

25 And, behold, there was a man in Jerusalem, whose name was Simeon; and the same man was just and devout, waiting for the consolation of Israel: and the Holy Ghost was upon him.

26 And it was revealed unto him by the Holy Ghost, that he should not see death, before he had seen the Lord's Christ.

27 And he came by the Spirit into the temple: and when the parents brought in the child Jesus, to do for him after the custom of the law,

28 Then took he him up in his arms, and blessed God, and said,

29 Lord, now lettest thou thy servant depart in peace, according to thy word:

30 For mine eyes have seen thy salvation,

31 Which thou hast prepared before the face of all people;

32 A light to lighten the Gentiles, and the glory of thy people Israel.

33 And Joseph and his mother marvelled at those things which were spoken of him.

34 And Simeon blessed them, and said unto Mary his mother, Behold, this child is set for the fall and rising again of many in Israel; and for a sign which shall be spoken against;

35 (Yea, a sword shall pierce through thy own soul also,) that the thoughts of many hearts may be revealed.

36 And there was one Anna, a prophetess, the daughter of Phanuel, of the tribe of Aser: she was of a great age, and had lived with an husband seven years from her virginity;

37 And she was a widow of about fourscore and four years, which departed not from the temple, but served God with fastings and prayers night and day.

38 And she coming in that instant gave thanks likewise unto the Lord, and spake of him to all them that looked for redemption in Jerusalem.

BIBLICAL DEFINITIONS

A. Devout (Luke 2:25) *eluabes* (Gk.)—Reverencing God, pious.
B. Glory (v. 32) *doxa* (Gk.)—The kingly majesty of the Messiah.
C. Redemption (v. 38) *lutrosis* (Gk.)—Ransoming, deliverance.

LIFE NEED FOR TODAY'S LESSON

AIM: Students will never lose hope in the promise of God.

INTRODUCTION

The Continuing Birth Story
After the announcement to the shepherds in **verses 8–20**, Luke skipped ahead eight days to the circumcision and naming of Jesus (**verse 21**). He was given the name Jesus, like the angel had told Mary and proclaimed to Joseph in a dream (**Luke 1:31; Matthew 1:21**). Mary had to undergo a purification ceremony 40 days after the birth of her son (**verse 22**; **Leviticus 12:1–4**). The purification ceremony included a sacrifice of a lamb and a pigeon, but exceptions were made for those who were poor. Impoverished Mary and Joseph could only offer two pigeons (or doves) (**verse 24**). Jesus was also presented to the Lord as the firstborn.

BIBLE LEARNING

AIM: Students will learn that God kept His promise to Simeon by allowing him to see the Messiah before Jesus was circumcised.

I. WAITING FOR THE MESSIAH (Luke 2:25–32)

Simeon was a "just and devout" Israelite, filled with the Holy Spirit. Though he was nearing the end of his life, Simeon believed God's promise through the Holy Spirit that he would not die before seeing Christ. Simeon believed the Old Testament prophecies and waited expectantly for "the consolation of Israel," the Messiah. All believers should faithfully trust God's promises in His Word.

Simeon's song of praise is called the *Nunc Dimittis*, which are the first two words in the Latin translation. The phrases he used were inspired by the Spirit and came in part from **Isaiah 40–55**. Simeon was ready to peacefully enter into eternal rest since he had beheld the Savior of all people, Jew and Gentile. Jesus would be "the glory of thy people Israel" because He was born a Jew and was first sent to them. Jesus would be "a light to lighten the Gentiles" by dispelling the darkness of sin and revealing a new way of life and salvation to those who had been excluded from God's covenant.

Simeon's Hope (verses 25–32)
25 And, behold, there was a man in Jerusalem, whose name was Simeon; and the same man was just and devout, waiting for the consolation of Israel: and the Holy Ghost was upon him. 26 And it was revealed unto him by the Holy Ghost, that he should not see death, before he had seen the Lord's Christ. 27 And he came by the Spirit into the temple: and when the parents brought in the child Jesus, to do for him after the custom of the law, 28 Then took he him up in his arms, and blessed God, and said, 29 Lord, now lettest thou thy servant depart in peace, according to thy word. 30 For mine eyes have seen thy salvation, 31 Which thou hast prepared before the face of all people. 32 A light to lighten the Gentiles, and the glory of thy

people Israel.

Luke cites four qualifications for Simeon, whose name means "God hears," which established him as a reliable witness in the eyes of traditional Jews. Liefeld observes, "It is appropriate that the Spirit who is the Consoler was upon one who awaited the consolation" (*Matthew, Mark, Luke. The Expositor's Bible Commentary,* 849). Naturally, Luke used the still-relevant Old Testament expression of the Holy Spirit being "upon" someone (e.g. **Numbers 11:17; Judges 3:10; 1 Samuel 10:6**), and similarly, referencing Jesus, "The spirit of the LORD shall rest upon him" (from **Isaiah 11:2**).

Simeon's divinely guided appointment. His moment of blessing or praise (Gk. *eulogeo*, **eu-lo-GE-oh**) was the perfect response to such a powerful, intimate meeting holding the infant Jesus in his arms while realizing the baby was the long-awaited Messiah. Simeon uttered a solemn poem of consecration (a psalm or song).

Luke used the word "Messiah," while Simeon used the metaphor "thy salvation." Liefeld wrote, "To see Jesus is to see salvation embodied in him" (*Matthew, Mark, Luke. The Expositor's Bible Commentary,* 849). The phrase about this salvation being prepared "before the face of all people" or "in the sight [or presence] of all people" in other versions, such as the NIV (cf. **Isaiah 52:10; Psalm 98:3**), implies the universality of the Gospel for God's salvation is intended for all mankind (see **Isaiah 42:6, 49:6**). The prophet's prayer, in David Jeffrey's words, "has been part of daily prayers since the fourth century.... Simeon's benedictional praise poem has.... become a 'sign to many' for two

millennia" (*Luke,* 47–48).

SEARCH THE SCRIPTURES

QUESTION

Describe Simeon based on **Luke 2:25**.

II. A JOYFUL SIGHT (Luke 2:36–38)

Anna was over 84 years old when the baby Jesus was presented in the temple and was so filled with joy when she saw the Messiah that she broke forth in praise. Like Simeon, she rejoiced in the fulfillment of the divine promises of God for her faithfulness had been rewarded. Then, she shared this Good News with others. All Christians should live by faith and strive for holiness for God will always honor His promises to those who remain faithful.

Anna's Devotion (verses 36–38)
36 And there was one Anna, a prophetess, the daughter of Phanuel, of the tribe of Aser: she was of a great age, and had lived with an husband seven years from her virginity. 37 And she was a widow of about fourscore and four years, which departed not from the temple, but served God with fastings and prayers nighgave thanks likewise unto the Lord, and spake of him to all them that looked for redemption in Jerusalem.

Anna, which means "favor," the second pious character to testify to Jesus' significance, was an elderly widow and "prophetess"—a familiar figure in both the Old and New Testaments (e.g. **Exodus 15:20; Judges 4:4; Acts 2:17**). Luke listed her tribal roots to bolster her authenticity as a Jewish witness.

That Anna "departed not from the

temple" as a holy woman; for the Temple was her life. Like Simeon, the Spirit led the prophetess by divine appointment to be present at the precise moment that Mary and Joseph brought baby Jesus to the Temple. Also, like Simeon, she both gave thanks and, considering her extreme devotion, offered a heartfelt speech for onlookers. J. C. Ryle perceptively comments, "When we read of Anna's consistency and holiness and prayerfulness and self-denial, we cannot but wish that many daughters of the Christian church would strive to be like her" (*Luke. The Crossway Classic Commentaries* 44).

Jesus' foundational grounding in the Mosaic Law from childhood (cf. **Galatians 4:4–5**) enabled Him later "to oppose flawed and hollow practices in the name of the Law of Moses," in the words of Fred Craddock (*Luke: Interpretation: A Bible Commentary for Teaching and Preaching,* 38). Jesus proved Simeon's prophetic words that many would speak against Him (**Luke 2:34**), and He would reveal the evil thoughts of many (**verse 35**). Through the ages, Jesus has continued to draw critics and reveal men's true thoughts, even while Simeon and Anna continue to testify that the Messiah brought salvation to all mankind. As Jesus Himself once pointedly asked, "Who do you say I am?" (**Matthew 16:15, NIV**).

SEARCH THE SCRIPTURES

QUESTION

Anna's response to seeing the child Jesus was to_____.

BIBLE APPLICATION

AIM: Students will continue to live holy lives while they await the fulfillment of God's promises.

Both Simeon and Anna lived holy lives as they faithfully served God. They were old when the promises of God were fulfilled concerning the Messiah. Simeon and Anna could have easily given up hope of ever seeing the Messiah in their lifetime, but they never doubted. True Christians can also live holy lives and await the fulfillment of God's promises. Every day, believers have to make a decision to trust and serve God in all types of circumstances.

STUDENTS' RESPONSES

AIM: Our devotion and service to God can draw others to Him.

God is calling us to a life of holiness. Age doesn't matter. Whether young or old, God wants His people to live as an example for others. How do we live holy lives? We can devote time to praying, fasting, and reading the Word. The Holy Spirit will help to sustain us. Our devotion and service to God can draw others to Him.

PRAYER

Lord, we thank you that no matter how long we wait, you fulfill your promises. We praise you because we can count on your Word. Father, we ask that you would help us to live holy lives while we wait on you. We pray that you would draw others to worship and serve you through our example of faith. In Jesus' name, we pray. Amen.

DIG A LITTLE DEEPER

It was known that day that Joseph and Mary were a poor couple. They were devout Jews who studied the Mosaic Law, i.e. standard behavior of Jewish customs. Even though we know that the law was given that declared them righteous; God knew that His people would not be able to keep all those laws so gave us Jesus; our Lord and Savior. The whole earth would be rumbling after the presentation of this baby. In the words of the sportscaster "Let's get reeaaaaady to rrrummmmble"!!! He will heal the brokenhearted, preach deliverance to the captives, recover the sight to the blind, set at liberty them that are bruised, and preach the acceptable year of the Lord. When Jesus' parents brought him into the temple to perform that which was customary, Simeon the priest received the revelation that he had been looking for! He blessed the baby Jesus and told Mary all the things He would do. He was so glad that he had seen and declared the identity of Jesus. Luke continues the theme of amazement through an old widow named Anna who had fasted and prayed in the Temple for 84 years. The scripture records "She did not leave the Temple" to say, she was there all the time. She confirmed the message of Simeon by giving thanks to God and speaking about this child to all those needing redemption. Jesus would be the light of men. "In Him was life and the light shineth in darkness; and the darkness would not understand him". (John 1:4-9)(NIV). These two people came as WITNESSES to "bear witness of the light, that all men through Him might be saved.

HOW TO SAY IT

Simeon. **SIM**-ih-un.

Phanuel. fuh-**NOO**-uhl.

Aser. **AY**-zer.

PREPARE FOR NEXT SUNDAY

Read **Luke 6:1–11** and study "Love, Mercy and The Sabbath."

Sources:
Bible Study Tools. www.BibleStudyTools.com. "Old Testament Hebrew Lexicon—King James Version." http://www.biblestudytools.com/lexicons/hebrew/kjv (accessed August 9, 2012).
Blue Letter Bible. BlueLetterBible.org. http://www.blueletterbible.org/ (accessed July 13, 2012).
Craddock, Fred B. *Luke: Interpretation: A Bible Commentary for Teaching and Preaching.* Louisville: John Knox Press, 1990. 28–40. Jamieson, Robert, A. R. Fausset, and David Brown. www.BibleStudyTools.com. *Commentary Critical and Explanatory on the Whole Bible.* http://www.biblestudytools.com/commentaries/jamieson-fausset-brown/luke/luke-2.html?p=5. (accessed August 10, 2012).
Jeffrey, David Lyle. *Luke.* Grand Rapids, MI: Brazos Press, 2012. 45–48.
Liefeld, Walter L. *Matthew, Mark, Luke. The Expositor's Bible Commentary, Vol. 8.* Edited by Frank E. Gaebelein. Grand Rapids, MI: Zondervan, 1984. 848–850.
Life Application Bible (NRSV). Wheaton, IL: Tyndale House, 1989. 1734–1745.
Ryle, J. C. *Luke. The Crossway Classic Commentaries.* Wheaton, IL: Crossway, 1997. 41–45.

DAILY HOME BIBLE READINGS

MONDAY
Parents Committed to the Law
(Luke 2:21–24)

TUESDAY
Circumcising on the Eighth Day
(Leviticus 12:1–5)

WEDNESDAY
Offering a Sacrifice to the Lord
(Leviticus 12:6–8)

THURSDAY
Consolation for Israel
(Isaiah 40:1–5)

FRIDAY
The Lord's Comfort and Compassion
(Isaiah 49:8–13)

SATURDAY
A Light to the Nations
(Isaiah 42:1–7)

SUNDAY
Jesus' Presentation in the Temple
(Luke 2:25–38)

LOVE, MERCY & THE SABBATH

BIBLE BASIS: LUKE 6:1—11

BIBLE TRUTH: Jesus is Lord of the Sabbath.

MEMORY VERSE: "Then said Jesus unto them, I will ask you one thing; Is it lawful on the sabbath days to do good, or to do evil? to save life, or to destroy it?" (Luke 6:9, KJV).

LESSON AIM: By the end of the lesson, we will: KNOW the Sabbath laws and their conflicts with human need; FEEL an appreciation for the priority of human needs being met; and DECIDE to live in such a way that we honor the Sabbath from Jesus' perspective.

BACKGROUND SCRIPTURES: John 5: 2-17— Read and incorporate the insights gained from the Background Scriptures into your study of the lesson.

LESSON SCRIPTURE

LUKE 6:1 – 11, KJV

1 And it came to pass on the second sabbath after the first, that he went through the corn fields; and his disciples plucked the ears of corn, and did eat, rubbing them in their hands.

2 And certain of the Pharisees said unto them, Why do ye that which is not lawful to do on the sabbath days?

3 And Jesus answering them said, Have ye not read so much as this, what David did, when himself was an hungred, and they which were with him;

4 How he went into the house of God, and did take and eat the shewbread, and gave also to them that were with him; which it is not lawful to eat but for the priests alone?

5 And he said unto them, That the Son of man is Lord also of the sabbath.

6 And it came to pass also on another sabbath, that he entered into the synagogue and taught: and there was a man whose right hand was withered.

7 And the scribes and Pharisees watched him, whether he would heal on the sabbath day; that they might find an accusation against him.

8 But he knew their thoughts, and said to the man which had the withered hand, Rise up, and stand forth in the midst. And he arose and stood forth.

9 Then said Jesus unto them, I will ask you one thing; Is it lawful on the sabbath days to do good, or to do evil? to save life, or to destroy it?

10 And looking round about upon them all, he said unto the man, Stretch forth thy hand. And he did so: and his hand was restored whole as the other.

11 And they were filled with madness; and communed one with another what they might do to Jesus.

BIBLICAL DEFINITIONS

A. Sabbath (Luke 6:1) *sabbaton* (Gk.)— The seventh day of each week, which was a sacred festival; on the Sabbath the Israelites were required to abstain from all work.

B. Do good (v. 9) *agathopoieo* (Gk.)—

35

To do something that helps or profits others.

LIFE NEED FOR TODAY'S LESSON

AIM: Students will learn acts of love and mercy are a part of the Sabbath.

INTRODUCTION

Work for the Sabbath

Work for the Sabbath observance was one of the marks of being a true Jew in first-century Palestine. True Sabbath observance was a controversial topic for it could mean not doing normal daily activities since there was no set definition of what was meant by "work." Pharisees and religious leaders debated the definition of "work" and established many guidelines to direct people in observing the Sabbath. Ordinary things were considered Sabbath violations like simply lighting a lamp. Unfortunately, many extra laws became direct violations of human need.

BIBLE LEARNING

AIM: Students will learn why good deeds can be a part of worship on the Sabbath.

I. HUNGER ON THE SABBATH (Luke 6:1–4)

This chapter in Luke was quite relatable because Jesus and His disciples were just hungry. Jesus broke a Sabbath rule causing the Pharisees to question him after he and His disciples plucked grains of corn, rubbed the grains in their hands, and ate the kernels. Jesus explained his actions by recounting a similar scriptural situation where David and his friends were also hungry running from King Saul. Although temple shewbread was reserved only for priests, wise Abiathar

the priest, fed them the shewbread and met their basic needs. This act of kindness showed how human needs were more of a priority than sticking to man-made rules.

Jesus went an extra step in meeting human needs by settling the debate on whether it was lawful to heal on the Sabbath by healing the man with the withered hand. He showed it was lawful to "do good" on the Sabbath and not to "do evil," to "save life" and not to "destroy it" (**verse 9**).

Jesus Meets Human Needs on the Sabbath (verses 1–4)

1 And it came to pass on the second sabbath after the first, that he went through the corn fields; and his disciples plucked the ears of corn, and did eat, rubbing them in their hands. 2 And certain of the Pharisees said unto them, Why do ye that which is not lawful to do on the sabbath days? 3 And Jesus answering them said, Have ye not read so much as this, what David did, when himself was an hungred, and they which were with him; 4 How he went into the house of God, and did take and eat the shewbread, and gave also to them that were with him; which it is not lawful to eat but for the priests alone?

Luke also highlighted how gleaning by hand and not using tools ("sickle," **Deuteronomy 23:25**) in someone else's field was permissible. The issue was the day of the week, which made what they were doing violations of just reaping, threshing, winnowing, and preparing food!

Jesus saw this as a teachable moment for the Pharisees so His example included David and His disciples with a similar controversy involving ritual law vs. moral law (**1 Samuel 21:1–6; cf. Exodus 25:30**). These teachers of the law had misunderstood their own scriptures. Today, it would be similar to Thomas Jefferson explaining the Constitution to the U.S. Supreme Court Justices or Bishop C.H. Mason explaining Church of God in Christ (COGIC) holiness principles to the COGIC General Board.

SEARCH THE SCRIPTURES

QUESTION

On the Sabbath, what did the disciples do?

II. AUTHORITY ON THE SABBATH (Luke 6:5)

Jesus intentionally shared the scriptural story of David and his men eating shewbread while they were on the run from King Saul. David had been anointed King of Israel but not yet crowned king. Using this story, Jesus is teaching another more important lesson by pointing out how He is the rightful King of Israel, although He is not king yet. This made His interpretation of keeping the Sabbath superior because He had authority as the rightful King of God's people. Jesus' actions on this Sabbath and His interpretations of the Sabbath are correct for He is Lord of the Sabbath.

Jesus is Lord of the Sabbath (verse 5)

5 And he said unto them, That the Son of man is Lord also of the sabbath.

The silence from the Pharisees as they heard Jesus make bold statements meant they did not have good answers. Jesus' straight-forward responses let them know without a doubt that He was divine

and had the authority to speak to the issues. His answers forced the Pharisees to see that He had not authored their interpretations of the fourth commandment because He created the original concept of the Sabbath, so He understood precisely what was and what was not permissible. We find Jesus, in J. C. Ryle's words, "clearing the day of God from the rubbish of human traditions" (Luke. The Crossway Classic Commentaries, 75).

III. HEALING AND MERCY ON THE SABBATH (Luke 6:6–10)

It was right and just for Jesus to allow His disciples to pluck and eat grain since they had a genuine need. They were hungry and the law allowed them to do it (**Deuteronomy 23:24–25**). It showed mercy to sympathize with hungry people. It showed mercy to heal on the Sabbath. The man with a withered hand received healing because it was right to do good and to save a life no matter what day it was. The man received healing because of Jesus' mercy toward him.

Jesus Shows Justice and Mercy on the Sabbath (verses 6–10)

6 And it came to pass also on another sabbath, that he entered into the synagogue and taught: and there was a man whose right hand was with ered. 7 And the scribes and Pharisees watched him, whether he would heal on the sabbath day; that they might find an accusation against him. 8 But he knew their thoughts, and said to the man which had the withered hand, Rise up, and stand forth in the midst. And he arose and stood forth. 9 Then said Jesus unto them, I will ask you one thing; Is it lawful on the sabbath days to do good, or to do evil?

to save life, or to destroy it? 10 And looking round about upon them all, he said unto the man, Stretch forth thy hand. And he did so: and his hand was restored whole as the other.

It would have been Jesus' custom from childhood to teach at the synagogue. Medically trained Doctor Luke noted details about Jesus' actions that other Gospel writers did not—for example, it was the man's right hand that was withered. Robert Stein describes this as "either paralysis or atro phy" (*Luke*, 189)—in other words, his primary hand was useless. Note also in those days, anyone left-handed was seen as weak or handicapped.

These straight-laced rabbis, law professors, and Jewish leaders shamelessly shadowed Jesus everywhere, like paparazzi or news media hounding presidential candidates or English royalty. They were on the prowl for any infraction to "find an accusa tion" (Heb. *kategoreo*, **ka-te-go-RE-o**). Per Stein, this meant "a legal accusation that could be used in court against Jesus" (*Luke. The New American Commentary*, 189); today, a formal, legal charge.

This illustrated how man's heart is hopelessly and helplessly evil (cf. **Genesis 6:5, 8:21; Jeremiah 17:9**). As the divine Son of man, Jesus "possessed a prophetic awareness of men's thoughts" (Stein, 190). Jesus helped to clarify His actions for He had the man stand up so everyone could get a good look at what was about to happen. John Phillips wrote that the Pharisees "had withered hearts that were as shriveled as the hand of the cripple" (*Exploring the Gospel of Luke*, 109)—He would have healed them, too, had they only reached out to Him. Jesus knew this was another perfect teachable moment from the scriptures. He shared two extremes, good/evil, save/destroy, which is "lawful"? Similar to today's phrase, "To not decide is to decide," evil is the default when good is withheld. If you have the ability and opportunity to do something good but do not do it, you actually do evil (**cf. James 4:17**). David Jeffrey notes "the law was intended to serve rather than to encumber the children of the covenant" (Luke, 86).

Luke's detailed narrative accurately captured Jesus' stage presence as He looked around before the healing, as if to make sure He had everyone's attention. At the command of the Lord of the Sabbath, the man's hand was restored and made whole again right before their eyes.

Luke's narrative eye for detail captured Jesus' stage presence as He looked around prior to the healing, as if to make sure He had everyone's attention. At the command of the Lord of the Sabbath, the man's hand was restored and made whole again right before their eyes.

SEARCH THE SCRIPTURES

QUESTION

Give an example of how Jesus challenged the Pharisees' thinking through His actions on the Sabbath?

IV. FREEDOM ON THE SABBATH (Luke 6:11)

Jesus claimed that the Sabbath was a means and not an end. The Pharisees had it all wrong. The Sabbath was a means to attain the end of doing good and showing justice and mercy. This is what people need for the Sabbath was not designed to oppress people but to liberate them and set them free.

Jesus Shows the True Meaning of the Sabbath (verse 11)

11 And they were filled with madness; and communed one with another what they might do to Jesus.

Instead of being amazed, impressed, or happy for the man; instead of allowing Jesus' good deed to rebuke their pettiness and self-centeredness—these leaders and teachers were irate! They were "out of their minds with anger," writes Jeffrey, not because of the good deed, but they were "enraged at being outwitted" (Luke, 89). Then, like the original sore losers, they agreed among themselves that something must be done to this impudent Jesus. Who did He think He was?

As with the confrontation just prior in **Luke 5:33– 39**, this one also illustrates the Pharisees' attempt to pour new wine (Jesus; new covenant) into old wineskins (Judaism; Mosaic covenant) and the resulting predictable problems (cf. **2 Corinthians 5:17**). Darrell Bock observes, "Jesus is bringing about the new era in which we now share . . . the new way means the end of the old way" (*Luke. The NIV Application Commentary,* 173).

The take-away is that God's children are still to honor the Sabbath, as God has commanded, but acts of kindness, mercy, and justice take priority over the letter of the law (cf. **Matthew 22:37– 40**). They can and should be done any time and, as the popular phrase goes, "twice on Sunday."

BIBLE APPLICATION

AIM: Students will meet human needs and overcome the rules and limitations that can become barriers to doing so.

There are numerous rules and limitations in our society that keep us from meeting human needs. Many times we will be challenged on whether to follow the rules or to follow justice and mercy. As followers of Christ, our allegiance is to our Lord of the Sabbath who is our Lord over the universe and every aspect of our lives. It is through following His example that we can meet human needs and overcome the rules and limitations that can become barriers. Jesus shows us that human needs are a priority over religious rule keeping. God's justice and mercy should be our guidelines when it comes to doing good and making a difference in the lives of others.

STUDENTS' RESPONSES

AIM: Students will begin trying to respond to human needs in the future better than they have in the past.

It can be hard to see the importance of human needs around us. Many times we are caught up in religious rule-keeping instead of the more important matter of showing justice and mercy to others. As followers of Jesus, we can learn from His example and bless those who are near us in tangible ways. We can choose to place ourselves in situations where human needs will be hard to ignore. We can volunteer at a soup kitchen or homeless shelter. We can also choose to ask more insightful questions of our brothers and sisters in Christ to assess any needs that they may have. Then, we can ask God for compassion to take action on the needs that He brings our way.

PRAYER

Father, we thank you for your Sabbath rest in Jesus. We praise you for being a God of love and mercy. We ask that you would empower us to show love and mercy to those who need it. Give us wisdom to discern when and how

39

we should act. In Jesus' name, we pray. Amen.

DIG A LITTLE DEEPER

On a Sabbath, while he was going through the grain field, Jesus and his disciples plucked and ate some heads of grain, rubbing them in their hands, and were accused of working on the Sabbath. John MacArthur in an article, 2018; ("To Save a Life Or Destroy It") outlined a portion of this absurdity. "He said, traveling more than 3,000 feet from home was forbidden on the Sabbath. But if one had placed food at the 3,000-foot point before the Sabbath, that point would then be considered home, since there was food there, which would allow the 3,000 feet of travel". They did not want to overstep their boundaries. Honoring the sabbath was an act of love for God's Holiness which was the law but it also reveals the love we should have for one another. One day out of every seventh day to stay focused on the Holiness of our God. However, Jesus felt that the keepers of the law misunderstood their teaching. Here is a boundary that should stick with us; "But whosoever has the world's goods and sees his brother in need and closes his heart against him, how does the love of God abide in him? Little children let us not love with word or with tongue, but in DEED and TRUTH. No matter how we spend the day, It is beneficial for us to spend the day in a relationship with God in any way we can.

HOW TO SAY IT

Shewbread. **SHOW**-bread.

Synagogue. **SI**-na-gog.

PREPARE FOR NEXT SUNDAY

Read **Luke 6:17–31** and study "Unconditional Love."

Sources:
Blue Letter Bible. BlueLetterBible.org. http://www.blueletterbible.org/ (accessed Friday, July 27, 2012).
Bock, Darrell L. *Luke. The NIV Application Commentary.* Grand Rapids, MI: Zondervan, 1996. 169–183.
Jeffrey, David Lyle. *Luke. Brazos Theological Commentary on the Bible.* Grand Rapids, MI: Brazos Press, 2012. 86–90.
Phillips, John. *Exploring the Gospel of Luke. The John Phillips Commentary Series.* Grand Rapids, MI: Kregel Academic and Professional, 2005. 108–110.
Ryle, J. C. *Luke. The Crossway Classic Commentaries.* Wheaton, IL: Crossway, 1997. 73–76.
Stein, Robert H. *Luke. The New American Commentary, Vol. 24.* Nashville: Holman Reference, 1992. 187–190.

COMMENTS / NOTES:

_____
_____
_____
_____

DAILY HOME BIBLE READINGS

MONDAY
God is Still Working
(John 5:2–17)

TUESDAY
A Day of Thanksgiving
(Psalm 92:1–8)

WEDNESDAY
A Day of Rest
(Exodus 16:22–30)

THURSDAY
A Day of Remembrance
(Deuteronomy 5:11–15)

FRIDAY
A Holy Convocation
(Leviticus 23:1–8)

SATURDAY
A Holy Day
(Jeremiah 17:19–27)

SUNDAY
Lord of the Sabbath
(Luke 6:1 – 11)

UNCONDITIONAL LOVE

BIBLE BASIS: Luke 6:17–31

BIBLE TRUTH: We may have to pay a price for our Christian witness.

MEMORY VERSE: "But I say unto you which hear, Love your enemies, do good to them which hate you" (Luke 6:27, KJV).

LESSON AIM: By the end of the lesson, we will: KNOW how to interpret the meanings of love and judgment; EXPLORE the difficult feelings associated with loving people who show total DISDAIN for us; and develop prayers that express love for the enemy.

BACKGROUND SCRIPTURES: Matthew 18:21-35 — Read and incorporate the insights gained from the Background Scriptures into your study of the lesson.

LESSON SCRIPTURE

LUKE 6:17–31, KJV

17 And he came down with them, and stood in the plain, and the company of his disciples, and a great multitude of people out of all Judaea and Jerusalem, and from the sea coast of Tyre and Sidon, which came to hear him, and to be healed of their diseases;

18 And they that were vexed with unclean spirits: and they were healed.

19 And the whole multitude sought to touch him: for there went virtue out of him, and healed them all.

20 And he lifted up his eyes on his disciples, and said, Blessed be ye poor: for yours is the kingdom of God.

21 Blessed are ye that hunger now: for ye shall be filled. Blessed are ye that weep now: for ye shall laugh.

22 Blessed are ye, when men shall hate you, and when they shall separate you from their company, and shall reproach you, and cast out your name as evil, for the Son of man's sake.

23 Rejoice ye in that day, and leap for joy: for, behold, your reward is great in heaven: for in the like manner did their fathers unto the prophets.

24 But woe unto you that are rich! for ye have received your consolation.

25 Woe unto you that are full! for ye shall hunger. Woe unto you that laugh now! for ye shall mourn and weep.

26 Woe unto you, when all men shall speak well of you! for so did their fathers to the false prophets.

27 But I say unto you which hear, Love your enemies, do good to them which hate you,

28 Bless them that curse you, and pray for them which despitefully use you.

29 And unto him that smiteth thee on the one cheek offer also the other; and him that taketh away thy cloak forbid not to take thy coat also.

30 Give to every man that asketh of thee; and of him that taketh away thy goods ask them not again.

31 And as ye would that men should do to you, do ye also to them likewise.

BIBLICAL DEFINITIONS

A. Blessed (Luke 6:20–22) *makarios* (Gk.)—Fortunate, happy.
B. Love (v. 27) *agapao* (Gk.)—To welcome, entertain, be fond of, love dearly, be full of goodwill and exhibit the same.

LIFE NEED FOR TODAY'S LESSON

AIM: Students will learn how to live as one of God's people amid opposition.

INTRODUCTION

The Sermon on the Plain

The Sermon on the Plain is one of the most powerful passages in the Bible for Jesus gives an agenda for God's Kingdom. He provides a set of rules and instructions for His people to live by. The first part of these instructions consists of four blessings and four woes. These blessings and woes are followed by specific instructions on loving our enemies and doing good to those who mistreat us. These instructions are general guidelines and do not cover every situation but can all be grouped under the Golden Rule: "Do to others as you would like them to do to you" (**6:31, NLT**).

BIBLE LEARNING

AIM: Students will learn what the Bible tells us about how God's people should respond to their enemies.

I. GOD'S BLESSINGS (Luke 6:17–23)

Jesus began His Sermon on the Plain by speaking blessings on those who follow Him because they are often the ones whom society considers outcast and downtrodden. Jesus turns the world's categories of blessedness upside-down by saying the poor, the hungry, the weeping, and the outcast are happy. Why are they happy? They are recipients of the kingdom and favor of God. It is not how much we possess or how many people praise us that matters. Our ultimate priority is receiving the praise of God. The pronouncements Jesus told the poor, outcast, and disabled crowd contain the empowerment needed to live distinctive lifestyles God calls us to live.

God's People are Recipients of God's Blessings (verses 17–23)

17 And he came down with them, and stood in the plain, and the company of his disciples, and a great multitude of people out of all Judaea and Jerusalem, and from the sea coast of Tyre and Sidon, which came to hear him, and to be healed of their diseases; 18 And they were vexed with unclean spirits: and they were healed. 19 And the whole multitude sought to touch him: for there went virtue out of him, and healed them all. 20 And he lifted up his eyes on his disciples, and said, Blessed be ye poor: for yours is the kingdom of God. 21 Blessed are ye that hunger now: for ye shall be filled. Blessed are ye that weep now: for ye shall laugh. 22 Blessed are ye, when men shall hate you, and when they shall

separate you from their company, and shall reproach you, and cast out your name as evil, for the Son of man's sake. 23 Rejoice ye in that day, and leap for joy: for, behold, your reward is great in heaven: for in the like manner did their father unto the prophets.

Note that Jesus "stood in the plain." Some translations say, "stood on a level place." The discourse that follows closely mirrors material in Matthew's Gospel, the Sermon on the Mount. Jesus may have shared the same sermon at two different locations, but even an elevated plateau above the sea of Galilee could be considered a "level place." Such a location would be ideal for the healing service that was about to take place in the upcoming verses.The word "virtue" (Gk., *dynamis*, **DOO-na-mis**) means strength, power, or ability. The English word "dynamite" comes from it and offers a wonderful word picture of what kind of power Jesus had among the people of the first century.

Jesus' Sermon on the Plain was much shorter than the Sermon on the Mount in Matthew (30 verses compared to 107 verses) Jesus goes through a series of blessings and woes starting with the poor. The word "happy" may best express the Greek word translated "blessed" (Gk., *markarioi*, **mar-KAY-rio**). When we think of the poor, we immediately think of those with material needs. But Luke is thinking from a different perspective. King David calls himself poor throughout the Old Testament (**Psalm 40:17; 86:1**), but he had material wealth as a king. Poor here is associated more with humility. It takes humility to

experience the Kingdom of God.

The hunger in this passage does appear to reference a physical hunger. And that hunger carries with it the promise to be filled—a theme in the Old Testament's treatment of a messianic banquet (cf. **Isaiah 25:6–9; Psalm 107:33–39**).

When Luke wrote his Gospel, many Jewish Christians were already being expelled from the synagogue, so it was a reality for his first-century readers. There was a time when the word "Christian" was a derogatory term (although it might even seem true today in some people's minds). Others would call Jesus' followers Christians, not to identify them, but to degrade them and hate them for their identification with Christ.

SEARCH THE SCRIPTURES QUESTIONS

1. What type of spirits did the people want Jesus to heal?

2. Complete the following Scripture: "And he lifted up, and said, be ye: for yours is the of God."

II. THE WORLD'S WOES (Luke 6:24–26)

Those who are regarded as blessed in this world have no reason to rejoice, for they have experienced all this life has to offer right now. The rich have all the comfort they will ever receive. The well-fed will be hungry. The laughing will be weeping. The universally praised will receive the fate of the false prophets of the Old Testament. They have their reward and have nothing to anticipate in the future.

God's People Anticipate Future

Rewards (verses 24–26)

But woe unto you that are rich! for ye have received your consolation. 25 Woe unto you that are full! for ye shall hunger. Woe unto you that laugh now! for ye shall mourn and weep. 26 Woe unto you, when all men shall speak well of you! for so did their fathers to the false prophets.

Here is a parallel list of woes that closely mirror the previous verses. Just as "poor" earlier was a reference to spiritual poverty, "rich" here means a sense of pride. It references someone with a haughty spirit. Throughout scripture, those with arrogant, haughty spirits are denounced (**Proverbs 28:6, 11; Isaiah 32:9– 14**). The comfort felt in this prideful arrogance is waning and unsustainable.

Jesus then continues to discuss those addressed by these woes. The source of their laughter is material and unlasting. The laughter is less about joy and more about looking down upon the fate of another. These people would eventually experience weeping and mourning. The tables would soon be turned. Luke goes on to record this situation later in the story of the rich man and Lazarus (**Luke 16:19–31**). We should be careful about the way we look at the fate of others and the attitude we display when another suffers a fate we feel they "deserve."

III. BLESSING FROM GOD'S PEOPLE (Luke 6:27–31)

Jesus' words to His followers are counter-cultural and counterintuitive. He commands us to do good to those who hate us, bless those who curse us, and pray for those who mistreat us. He commands us to turn the other cheek to those who strike us and to give to those who take from us.

Jesus also gives one last guideline that includes the previous commands and sums up the main way that His followers will live a distinctive lifestyle: "Do to others as you would like them to do to you" (**verse 31, NLT**). It is the guiding principle of seeking another's goodwill.

If it were changed to "do to others as they have done to you," there would be room for retaliation and revenge. However, Jesus' command draws on our own desire for well-being so we transfer that to our fellow man no matter what he has done to us. This is the main characteristic of living a distinctive lifestyle as a follower of Christ.

God's People are Called to Live a Distinctive Lifestyle (verses 27–31)

27 But I say unto you which hear, Love your enemies, do good to them which hate you, 28 Bless them that curse you, and pray for them which despitefully use you. 29 And unto him that smiteth thee on thee cheek offer also the other; and him that taketh away thy cloke forbid not to take thy coat also. 30 Give to every man that asketh of thee, and of him that taketh away thy goods ask them not again. 31 And as ye would that men should do to you, do ye also to them likewise.

It's important to note the opening word, "but," which serves to separate the verse from the woes listed just prior (**verses 24–26**). The woes did not apply to the disciples, because Jesus counted them among those who both listened to His teachings and heard them—they had ears to hear (cf. **Luke 8:8, 14:35; Romans 11:8**). The teaching opens by zeroing in on the last beatitude (**verse 22**; cf. **Matthew 5:38–48**). Robert Stein observes, "Jesus' positive emphasis on loving your enemies is unique in its clarity as well as in the numerous examples given to explain what this love entails" (*Luke*, 206).

DIG A LITTLE DEEPER

How would you like to be back in Jesus' day when he taught with authority and revealed the plan of salvation for the lives of every believer? In Jesus' time, there were many poor and many sick, many outcasts and many afflicted; in which the beatitudes presented to them the grace of God. How prolific were the instructions given by Jesus letting us know that we were blessed and how to be blessed? Blessed simply means to be happy, to be envied, to be well-liked. But by the same token Jesus flipped the script. WOE is a very stern word that brings on distress. We all love great sermons; especially sermons filled with how God can do the impossible. When the sermon takes another turn we must subscribe to take the bitter with the sweet. God's word even though it is filled with grace it is also; "quick, and powerful, and sharper … and is a discerner of the thoughts and intents of the heart" *(Heb. 4:12).(KJV)*. Jesus knew that we all need lessons in our attitude, our gratitude, our love walk, and our expression of faith. To do this every area of our lives should be addressed. It is called spiritual discipline.

PREPARE FOR NEXT SUNDAY

Read **Luke 14:7-18a, 22-24** and study Godly Relationships.

COMMENTS / NOTES:

_____
_____
_____
_____
_____
_____

DAILY HOME BIBLE READINGS

MONDAY
Judge by the Righteous God
(Psalm 7:7–17)

TUESDAY
The Righteoud and Upright
(Proverbs 11:3–11)

WEDNESDAY
Enslaved to God
(Romans 6:16–23)

THURSDAY
Living as God's Servants
(1 Peter 2:11–17)

FRIDAY
Forgiveness and Mercy
(Matthew 18:21–35)

SATURDAY
Blessings and Woes
(Luke 6:20–26)

SUNDAY
Do Not Judge
(Luke 6:27–42)

GODLY RELATIONSHIPS

BIBLE BASIS: LUKE 14:7–18a, 22–24

BIBLE TRUTH: God exalts the humble.

MEMORY VERSE: "But I say unto you which hear, Love your enemies, do good to them which hate you" (Luke 6:27, KJV).

LESSON AIM: By the end of the lesson, we will: EXPLORE Jesus' teachings about humility and exaltation; EVALUATE attitudes and behavior toward those who are disenfranchised; and SEEK ways to invite people who do not normally participate in the local church.

BACKGROUND SCRIPTURES: Psalm 147:1–11, Luke 14:1-6 — Read and incorporate the insights gained from the Background Scriptures into your study of the lesson.Scriptures into your study of the lesson.

LESSON SCRIPTURE

LUKE 14:7 – 18a, 22-24, KJV

7 And he put forth a parable to those which were bidden, when he marked how they chose out the chief rooms; saying unto them.

8 When thou art bidden of any man to a wedding, sit not down in the highest room; lest a more honourable man than thou be bidden of him;

9 And he that bade thee and him come and say to thee, Give this man place; and thou begin with shame to take the lowest room.

10 But when thou art bidden, go and sit down in the lowest room; that when he that bade thee cometh, he may say unto thee, Friend, go up higher: then shalt thou have worship in the presence of them that sit at meat with thee.

11 For whosoever exalteth himself shall be abased; and he that humbleth himself shall be exalted.

12 Then said he also to him that bade him, When thou makest a dinner or a supper, call not thy friends, nor thy brethren, neither thy kinsmen, nor thy rich neighbours; lest they also bid thee again, and a recompence be made thee.

13 But when thou makest a feast, call the poor, the maimed, the lame, the blind:

14 And thou shalt be blessed; for they cannot recompense thee: for thou shalt be recompensed at the resurrection of the just.

15 And when one of them that sat at meat with him heard these things, he said unto him, Blessed is he that shall eat bread in the kingdom of God.

16 Then said he unto him, A certain man made a great supper, and bade many:

17 And sent his servant at supper time to say to them that were bidden, Come; for all things are now ready.

18 And they all with one consent began to make excuse.

22 And the servant said, Lord, it is done as thou hast commanded, and yet there is room.

23 And the lord said unto the servant, Go out into the highways and hedges, and compel them to come in, that my house may be filled.

24 For I say unto you, That none of those men which were bidden shall taste of my supper.

BIBLICAL DEFINITIONS

A. Humble (Luke 14:11, NLT) *tapeinoo* (Gk.)—To make low.
B. Exalt (v. 11, NLT) *hupsoo* (Gk.)—To rise to dignity, honor, and happiness.

LIFE NEED FOR TODAY'S LESSON

AIM: **Students will learn how to treat visitors to church.**

INTRODUCTION

Conflict with the Pharisees

Jesus was always in conflict with the Pharisees for their teachings and hypocrisy. In **Luke 12**, Jesus warned the people against false doctrine (**verses 1–3**). The teachings of the empty ritualists, the Pharisees, were nothing but a sham and hypocrisy. Jesus used the parable of the rich fool to express a warning against covetousness (**verses 16–21**). He wants us to seek the spiritual benefits of the kingdom rather than the material goods of the world.

In **chapter 13**, Jesus taught on repentance and judging (**13:1–5**). This contradicted the Pharisees' teaching that salvation comes from strict obedience to the law, not the forgiveness of sins. On His way to Jerusalem, Jesus was warned by the Pharisees that Herod Antipas wanted to kill Him. However,

the Pharisees said this to frighten Him into leaving the area. Jesus told them to tell Herod that His life's purpose was predetermined, and no one could change it. He wept over the condition of the people in Jerusalem (**verses 31–35**).

In **chapter 14**, Jesus was invited to a Pharisee leader's house for a meal on the Sabbath (**verse 1**). This was not the first time He had been invited to a Pharisee's house (**7:36**). On this occasion, the Pharisees and lawyers present invited Jesus to the Sabbath meal to watch if He would say or do something so they could arrest Him. A man with dropsy (swelling under the skin) was present so Jesus questioned the Pharisees about the lawfulness of healing a man on the Sabbath. There was no response so Jesus healed him (**14:2-4**). This didn't violate Sabbath laws, just the Pharisees' interpretation.

BIBLE LEARNING

AIM: **Students will learn that Jesus warns about always seeking the place of honor.**

I. HOW TO BE EXALTED (Luke 14:7–11)

The Pharisees watched Jesus and He also watched them. He noticed how guests chose the best seats at the table (**verse 7**). The places of honor were the middle seats where the most important guests sat. Some felt it was vital that they sit in places of honor. This gave the symbolic status of being important.

The Places of Honor (verses 7–11)

7 And he put forth a parable to those which were bidden, when he marked how they chose out the chief rooms; saying unto them, **8** When thou art bidden of any man to a wedding, sit not down in the highest room; lest a

more honourable man than thou be bidden of him. 9 And he that bade thee and him come and say to thee, Give this man place; and thou begin with shame to take the low est room. 10 But when thou art bidden, go and sit down in the lowest room; that when he that bade thee cometh, he may say unto thee, Friend, go up higher: then shalt thou have worship in the presence of them that sit at meat with thee. 11 For whosoever exalteth himself shall be abased; and he that humbleth himself shall be exalted.

A key term in this passage is "bidden" (Gk.*kaleo*, **kal-EH-o**), which is also the word for "invite," "summon" and "call." The root of the verb "to invite" or "call" appears ten times in the lesson. Jesus was speaking of those who were called to be His disciples and to whom He was giving instructions in the form of a parable, as well as those literally invited to dinner as guests.

Jesus was at a dinner with the disciples when He commanded them to observe where guests at a feast were choosing to sit. Jesus called forth imagery from the wisdom tradition found in the proverbs (cf. **Proverbs 25:6–7**) to teach the disciples about how one who is called should act humbly. He began the parable with a reference to the seating order at chief rooms (Gk. *protoklisia*, **pro-tok-li SEE-ah**) or places of honor at a banquet.

The custom in antiquity was that the most distinguished (Gk. *entimos*, **EN-tee-mos**) guests at a dinner or feast arrived late and reclined at the space at the table (Gk. *kataklino*, **kat-ak-LEE-no**) closest to the host. Jesus admonished the disciples not to be like the other guests vying to sit in the places of honor before all the other guests arrived because someone of higher social status might still come.

Honor and shame were very real concepts in the ancient Near East. Honor has a positive value for males, and modesty (Gk. *aischyne*, **ahee-SKHOO nay**) has a positive value for women. Shame is a negative value for men and represents a loss of manliness. The man forced to move from the privileged seat at the head of the table down to the lowest (Gk. *eschatos*, **ES-khat-os**) end in front of all the other guests would not only be shamed by being relocated but also because he had assumed a position in society to which he did not belong.

By contrast, Jesus commanded the disciples not to follow the example of the other guests but to do the unexpected and show humility by sitting at the farthest end of the banquet table. The expectation was that the host would seat the honored guests who arrived late at the front of the table near himself. However, the one who invited them has the prerogative to seat the guests wherever he chooses and may invite the guest with the lowest social status to move up to the higher (Gk. *anoteros*, **an-O ter-os**) place of honor.

The Greek word for "worship" is *doxa* (**DOX-ah**) and means "glory." It is a term usually reserved for God. However, in the Hebrew and Greco-Roman context, it means the enhancement of one's reputation or social status. The act of seating the guest of more modest stature at the higher end would signal to the other guests that this person had moved up the ranks and was now worthy of honor.

The real lesson Jesus was trying to impart to the disciples is that in God's Kingdom, God will bring about a reversal of human social constructs. The ones considered among the lowest socially will be exalted or lifted up, and those who have enjoyed the highest social position, either as a result of the family they were born into or wealth acquired legitimately or through schemes, will be lowered.

SEARCH THE SCRIPTURES

QUESTION

Jesus told a disciple to convey his message to the invited dinner guests.

II. WHOM TO INVITE (Luke 14:12–14)

Jesus observed the behavior of His host and gave some advice. He suggested that when a host has a special meal, he should not invite only friends, family, or rich neighbors, for they can reciprocate the invitation or grant favors. Instead, he should invite the poor, needy, and sick because they have no way to repay. They have no property or place in society, but they will pray for God's blessings upon the host for such kindness and hospitality.

The Invitations (verses 12–14)
12 Then said he also to him that bade him, When thou makest a dinner or a supper, call not thy friends, nor thy brethren, neither thy kinsmen, nor thy rich neighbours; lest they also bid thee again, and a recompence be made thee. 13 But when thou makest a feast, call the poor, the maimed, the lame, the blind. 14 And thou shalt be blessed; for they cannot recompense thee: for thou shalt be recompensed at the resurrection of the just.

Jesus next turned His attention to the host. One scholar noted that the host, like the guests, was more concerned with social status than the needs of those lower on the social rung. Jesus addressed this by advising him that when he prepared dinner, he should not exclusively invite his friends, siblings, extended family members, or neighbors who had an exceeding abundance of material wealth and would be obligated to invite him to dinner in kind. The Greek word for "recompence" (*antapodoma*, **an-tap-OD-om-ah**) means repayment. In the ancient world, gift-giving was reciprocal and built relationships between the giver and receiver, therefore creating solidarity. However, a poor person could not repay a rich person who invited the poor person to dine, a fact that would have been obvious to the host.

In a reversal of societal expectations, Jesus commanded His host to instead invite the poor, the physically disabled, and the blind. The poor, maimed, lame, and blind were members of society who were dependent on public generosity for their welfare and did not have the financial resources to repay their host. Jesus counseled the host that he should extend an invitation to society's outcasts.

Jesus was very concerned with those pushed to the margins of society because of their economic disadvantage, uncleanness, or physical disability.

Jesus' message is that performing such acts of kindness without the expectation for a reward would not only bless the individual here on earth but he or she would receive a heavenly reward at the resurrection of the just (cf. **Daniel 12:2–3**).

SEARCH THE SCRIPTURES

QUESTION

Jesus tells the Pharisees that their guest

list should include who? Is this guest list reflected in your church's ministry and in your family?

III. JESUS' MEANING
(Luke 14:15–18a, 22–24)

Jesus was using this parable to relate kingdom principles. The self-righteous (unbelieving Jews), especially the Pharisees, made excuses to get out of attending the great supper of salvation provided by God. They rejected Jesus' claims of being the Messiah and the need for His death on the Cross for the forgiveness of sins. Since they refused to accept the invitation, the invitation was extended to other people (disenfranchised of Israel and Gentiles) to replace the original guests (unbelieving Jews, **verse 24**). All those who accept will be welcomed into God's Kingdom.

The Parable of the Great Banquet
(verses 14:15–18a, 22–24)

15 And when one of them that sat at meat with him heard these things, he said unto him, Blessed is he that shall eat bread in the kingdom of God. 16 Then said he unto him, A certain man made a great supper, and bade many. 17 And sent his servant at supper time to say to them that were bid den, Come; for all things are now ready. 18a And they all with one consent began to make excuse. 22 And the servant said, Lord, it is done as thou hast commanded, and yet there is room. 23 And the lord said unto the servant, Go out into the highways and hedges, and compel them to come in, that my house may be filled. 24 For I say unto you, That none of those men which were bidden shall taste of my supper.

Jesus' remarks on the resurrection of the just prompted one of the guests to comment that one would be happy to eat bread in the Kingdom of God. The Greek word for "bread" (*artos*, **AR-tos**) means literally the bread one eats, and figuratively, the sustenance provided by God. The guest was implying that on the occasion of the resurrection of the just, one would enjoy his or her fill of food, thus experiencing a state of happiness. His remark allowed Jesus to introduce a parable on the great messianic banquet in the Kingdom (Gk. *basileia*, **bas-il-I-ah**) of God.

Jesus began the parable of the kingdom by telling the story of a wealthy man who prepared a lot of food for an evening meal (Gk. *deipnon*, **DIPE-non**) and invited enough people to share it with him. He assumed and took for granted that an invitation from him would have been positively received, as the above reference to **Matthew 22:1–10**.

The man sent his servant (Gk. *doulos*, **DOO-los**) to tell the invited guests that preparations were ready (Gk. *hetoimos*, **het-OY-mos**) and it was time to come eat. It is inferred that they had already received their invitations, and the time had come to accept. The summons by the servant reflects an ancient upper-class Jewish and Roman practice as a courtesy to the guests. Some scholars suggest the parable refers to salvation, and Jesus is saying that the Kingdom of God is at hand. The gracious host is God, who extended the invitation of salvation first to Israel, then to the rest of the nations.

To say that all the guests rejected the summons to dinner with one accord or as one (Gk. *mias*, **MI-as**) voice implies that an entire group of people rejected the offer of salvation. We should be careful not to interpret this to suggest that, for example, all Jewish people or all wealthy people rejected salvation. The main point is that those to whom the invitation was first extended refused. Therefore, salvation was extended to others, and finally to those least expected. This is not so hard to imagine. Sometimes the people whom we believe have the most need for a helping hand will refuse because of who is offering assistance.

The master (*kyrios*, **KOO-ree-os**) compelled the servant to search everywhere for anyone to bring to his house. The Greek word for "compel" (*anag kazo*, **an-ang-KAD-so**) in this situation means to do something with urgency. It implies an impending situation that requires immediate attention. God will do everything possible to reach each person because time is of the essence.

Jesus concluded the parable by saying that the original guests who declined the invitation will have passed on the opportunity to share in the man's meal. Consequently, if we who are called refuse the opportunity to follow Jesus and become His disciples, we will not taste (Gk. *geumai*, **GHYOO om-ahee**) or experience the messianic banquet that is to come.

BIBLE APPLICATION

AIM: Students will be motivated to practice acceptance and hospitality to all people.

One of the greatest obstacles to reaching the disenfranchised is our misconception about others. Some of it may be our feelings of superiority. Or, we just do not want "those types of people" in our congregations. Whatever the reasoning, it is not acceptable to Christ. He wants us to practice hospitality and welcome all people. After all, His kingdom will be composed of people from "every kindred, and tongue, and people, and nation" (**Revelation 5:9**).

STUDENTS' RESPONSES

AIM: Students will pay close attention to how they conduct themselves as invited guests.

This week, evaluate what is hindering you from inviting others to your church. Pray and ask God to forgive you for letting it stop you from witnessing and welcoming others. Discuss with your church leader and other members how to show hospitality and reach out to the disenfranchised in your communities. This can include community parties, health clinics, food programs, door-to-door witnessing, community concerts, etc.

PRAYER

Father, we praise you because you have the highest honor in the universe. We all must humbly submit to your greatness. We ask that you show us how to love and welcome all people.

We pray that you would give us hearts that seek to give honor and not receive honor. In Jesus' name we pray. Amen.

DIG A LITTLE DEEPER

What's more important the people at the party or the food? I would say the food but to Jesus, the people were of the most importance, and the position and status of the people were even more important. Christ taught the spirit of humility not because he was lesser of a man. He always esteemed others more highly than himself. Initially, this is the way we should live. Jesus wants to know what would we give up to gain and save to lose. The pride of the Pharisees was to have the chief seats but teaching humility teaches us how to serve others. *John 13:12-15 (KJV).* *"So when He had washed their feet, taken His garments, and sat down again, He said to them, "Do you know what I have done to you? You call me Teacher and Lord, and you say well, for so I am. If I then, your Lord and Teacher, have washed your feet, you also ought to wash one another's feet. For I have given you an example, that you should do as I have done to you."* Therefore the place of honor should be in our hearts.

HOW TO SAY IT

Recompensed. re-**KAM**-pents. Resurrection. re-ze-**REK**-shun.

PREPARE FOR NEXT SUNDAY

Read **Luke 16:19–31** and study "Compassion For the Poor."

Sources
Bauer, Walter, William F. Arndt, F. Wilbur Gingrich, and Frederick W. Danker. *A Greek-English Lexicon of the New Testament and Other Early Christian Literature, Second Edition.* Chicago: University of Chicago Press, 1979.
Bible Study Tools. www.BibleStudyTools.com. Bakers Evangelical Dictionary. "Hospitality." http://www.biblestudytools.com/ dictionaries/bakers-evangelical-dictionary/hospitality.html
Bible Study Tools. "Hupsoo—New Testament Greek Lexicon—King James Version." http://www.biblestudytools.com/ lexicons/ greek/kjv/hupsoo.html (accessed August 16, 2012).
Bible Study Tools. "Tapeinoo—New Testament Greek Lexicon—King James Version." http://www.biblestudytools.com/ lexicons/ greek/kjv/tapeinoo.html (accessed August 16, 2012).
Craddock, Fred B. *Luke: Interpretation: A Bible Commentary for Teaching and Preaching.* Louisville: John Knox Press, 1990, 169–183. Freeman, David. "Poor, Poverty." *Anchor Bible Dictionary.* New York: Doubleday, 1992, 403–424.
Gilmore, David, ed. *Honor and Shame and the Unity of the Mediterranean.* Washington, DC: American Anthropological Association, 1987. Gill, John. www.BibleStudyTools.com. "John Gill's Exposition of the Bible. Luke 14." http://www. biblestudytools.com/ commentaries/gills-exposition-of-the-bible/luke-14.html (accessed August 26, 2012).
Life Application Bible (NRSV). Wheaton, IL: Tyndale House, 1989. 1781–1786.
Marshall, I. Howard. *The Gospel of Luke. New International Greek Testament Commentary.* Grand Rapids, MI: Wm. B. Eerdmans Publishing Co., 1978.
Mauss, Marcel. *The Gift: Forms and Functions of Exchange in Archaic Societies.* Cohen & West, 1954.

COMMENTS / NOTES:

_____
_____
_____
_____
_____
_____
_____
_____

DAILY HOME BIBLE READINGS

MONDAY
The Danger of Self-Exaltation
(Isaiah 14:12–20)

TUESDAY
Humble Yourself Before the Lord
(James 4:7–12)

WEDNESDAY
God Gives Grace to the Humble
(1 Peter 5:1–7)

THURSDAY
God Gathers the Outcasts
(Psalm 147:1–11)

FRIDAY
God Lifts the Poor and Needy
(Psalm 113)

SATURDAY
God Shows No Partiality
(Romans 2:1–11)

SUNDAY
Honor and Disgrace
(Luke 14:7–18a, 22–24)

COOMPASSION FOR THE POOR

BIBLE BASIS: LUKE 16:19–31

BIBLE TRUTH: Compassion and generosity are important Christian values.

MEMORY VERSE: "He that is faithful in that which is least is faithful also in much: and he that is unjust in the least is unjust also in much" (Luke 16:10, KJV).

LESSON AIM: By the end of the lesson, we will: REVIEW the story of the rich man and Lazarus; DISCUSS our feelings about compassion toward the poor; and CONSIDER involving our congregation in developing a project that addresses selfishness and has a positive effect on everyone's attitudes and actions toward the poor.

BACKGROUND SCRIPTURES: Luke 19:1-10 — Read and incorporate the insights gained from the Background Scriptures into your study of the lesson.

LESSON SCRIPTURE

LUKE 16:19–31, KJV

19 There was a certain rich man, which was clothed in purple and fine linen, and fared sumptuously every day:

20 And there was a certain beggar named Lazarus, which was laid at his gate, full of sores,

21 And desiring to be fed with the crumbs which fell from the rich man's table: moreover the dogs came and licked his sores.

22 And it came to pass, that the beggar died, and was carried by the angels into Abraham's bosom: the rich man also died, and was buried;

23 And in hell he lift up his eyes, being in torments, and seeth Abraham afar off, and Lazarus in his bosom.

24 And he cried and said, Father Abraham, have mercy on me, and send Lazarus, that he may dip the tip of his finger in water, and cool my tongue; for I am tormented in this flame.

25 But Abraham said, Son, remember that thou in thy lifetime receivedst thy good things, and likewise Lazarus evil things: but now he is comforted, and thou art tormented.

26 And beside all this, between us and you there is a great gulf fixed: so that they which would pass from hence to you cannot; neither can they pass to us, that would come from thence.

27 Then he said, I pray thee therefore, father, that thou wouldest send him to my father's house:

28 For I have five brethren; that he may testify unto them, lest they also come into this place of torment.

29 Abraham saith unto him, They have Moses and the prophets; let them hear them.

30 And he said, Nay, father Abraham: but if one went unto them from the dead, they will repent.

31 And he said unto him, If they hear not Moses and the prophets, neither will they be persuaded, though one rose from the dead

BIBLICAL DEFINITIONS

A. Rich (Luke 16:19) *plousios* (Gk.)— Wealthy, abounding with.
B. Beggar (v. 20) *ptochos* (Gk.)—Poor and helpless; one who in his abjectness needs lifting.

LIFE NEED FOR TODAY'S LESSON

AIM: Students would not measure people by what they do and what they have.

INTRODUCTION

God Reads the Heart

Jesus declared that the Kingdom of God runs counter to the dominant culture. The Pharisees relished their wealth and power, but Jesus warned them that they fell short of God's standards. He bruised their egos by letting them know God reads the heart, so it was useless to justify themselves based on their works (**verse 15**).

BIBLE LEARNING

AIM: Students will learn the importance of sharing what we have with the less fortunate.

I. TWO DISPARATE LIVES (Luke 16:19–21)

Jesus introduced Lazarus, a homeless beggar who stayed at the gate. As a part of the lowest social caste, he relied on the mercy and kindness of others to receive crumbs to eat. Unlike the rich man, his existence was survival mode, he was unhealthy and malnourished. His clothes were tattered and worn. He lived in constant pain from sores that covered his body. As an outcast, the only touch he received was from the dogs who licked his wounds. Lazarus lived in a constant state of need. Jesus took time and care to set up this story to communicate a message that is consistent with God's love and care for the poor and His disdain for those who would mistreat them. In establishing the Children of Israel as a nation, God always made provision to care for the poor, widows, orphans, those enslaved due to debt, and foreigners (**Exodus 22:21–24; Leviticus 23:22; Deuteronomy 15:4–8, 11**). God commands His people to be a blessing to those in need and to show the same compassion He has shown. Their abundance was never meant to be hoarded but to be given freely so that no one would be in lack.

A Picture of Life (verses 19–21)

19 There was a certain rich man, which was clothed in purple and fine linen, and fared sumptuously every day. 20 And there was a certain beggar named Lazarus, which was laid at his gate, full of sores, 21 And desiring to be fed with the crumbs which fell from the rich man's table: moreover the dogs came and licked his sores.

Purple was a royal color in Jesus' time, like the purple "kingly" robe mockingly tossed around His bleeding body to match his "crown" of thorns (**John**

19:2, 5). Lydia was a dealer in purple cloth (**Acts 16:14**). Fine linens refer to high-quality undergarments made in Egypt. The ESV and RSV both have "feasted sumptuously," although "fared" (Gk. *euphraino*, **yu-FRI-no**) essentially means to celebrate or make merry, as in "eat, drink, and be merry" (**Luke 12:19**), which clearly includes feasting. A familiar concept in any time period, the set up of the parable clearly is a person living in the lap of luxury and enjoying the finest of everything.

Unique among all of Jesus' parables, here He named one of His characters. When Jesus named the poor man and left the rich man unnamed this shows the most important figure in the story since, normally, the rich would be named and the poor would be nameless. Dr. Luke's use of "sores," meaning ulcerations, in one of the few instances in scripture with the single use of a Greek or Hebrew word not repeated elsewhere (Gk. *helkoo*, **hel-KO-o**). Since the man was "full of sores" indicates a truly pitiful state.

SEARCH THE SCRIPTURES QUESTIONS

What did Lazarus want from the rich man?

II. HEAVEN AND HELL (Luke 16:22–26)

Jesus gave us dramatic detail of the rich man's torment as he sought to receive just a drop of water because of the intense heat of the flames. Abraham reminded the rich man of the life he lived on earth and how he had everything while Lazarus had lived in lack, constant pain, and shame. Now the roles had been reversed: Lazarus was in

comfort and the rich man was in agony. One could argue the rich man had a lot of nerve wanting Lazarus to relieve his agony when he showed no compassion to Lazarus while on earth, but God shows us through Jesus that He will always care for the poor, and the selfish will receive their just reward (**Psalm 147:6**). Abraham spoke to the rich man, noting that there was a gulf or chasm separating them so no one could pass between.

Hannah provided a similar picture in her prayer about God's justice for the poor: "They that were full have hired out themselves for bread; and they that were hungry ceased . . . He raiseth up the poor out of the dust, and lifteth up the beggar from the dunghill, to set them among princes, and to make them inherit the throne of glory: for the pillars of the earth are the LORD's, and he hath set the world upon them" (**1 Samuel 2:5, 8**).

A Picture of the Afterlife (verses 22–26)

22 And it came to pass, that the beggar died, and was carried by the angels into Abraham's bosom: the rich man also died, and was buried; 23 And in hell he lift up his eyes, being in torments, and seeth Abraham afar off, and Lazarus in his bosom. 24 And he cried and said, Father Abraham, have mercy on me, and send Lazarus, that he may dip the tip of his finger in water, and cool my tongue; for I am tormented in this flame. 25 But Abraham said, Son, remember that thou in thy lifetime receivedst thy good things, and likewise Lazarus evil things: but now he is comforted, and thou art tormented. 26 And beside all this,

between us and you there is a great gulf fixed: so that they which would pass from hence to you can not; neither can they pass to us, that would come from thence.

In the reversal, angels escorted the once lowly Lazarus to Abraham's bosom or side (Gk. *kolpos*, **KOL-pos**), which is the ultimate contentment for believing Jews (cf. **Matthew 8:11**)—"a poetic description of heaven," writes Philips, adding, "at death we are not left to find our own way home" (*Exploring the Gospel of Luke,* 220). For other uses of the same Greek word, Jesus was in the Father's bosom (**John 1:18**), and John leaned on Jesus' bosom (**John 13:23**). No one really knows what happens on the other side, but it is comforting that Jesus provided a picture of a gracious escort. For those who manage to escape judgment for their evil deeds in this life, it is also comforting to know that they will not escape ultimate justice. Paul tells us that those believers who fall asleep are with Christ (**2 Corinthians 5:8; Philippians 1:23**). In contrast, biological Jews are not guaranteed a place at Abraham's bosom by their bloodline alone—rather, along with the rest of unrepentant humanity, they also will face divine judgment.

Lazarus' reunion with Abraham contrasted with his previous life with dogs for company. The rich man's former luxury ended and was replaced with torment—a more serious condition than Lazarus' former humiliation. Lazarus' new reality of blessing also placed him with patriarchs of the faith (cf. **John 8:39**), much like the modern future hope of being rejoined with loved ones as well

as saints who passed before. The reversal continued with Lazarus' future in heaven compared with the rich man's opposite future in hell (Gk. *hades*, **HA-das**), which is the "lower parts of the earth" (**Ephesians 4:9**). Craddock describes this as the "flames of Hades" (*Luke,* 196). In life, the rich man was blessed and Lazarus suffered, but both temporarily. In death, Lazarus was blessed and the rich man suffered, now eternally (cf. the contrasts of the poor versus the rich in the Beatitudes, **Luke 6:20–26**). Whatever hell actually looks like, clearly there is terrible torment, and fire is a perfect depiction.

Jesus' message to the Pharisees is clear: Just as the rich man was fatally wrong to ignore Lazarus and have no compassion on him, so the Pharisees were just as fatally wrong in their self-righteous and cold-hearted lifestyle. Other Old Testament laws pointed to having mercy on the poor and transients (e.g., **Leviticus 19:9–10; Deuteronomy 15:7–11** even speaking of a gate like the rich man's). In fact, **Isaiah 58:6–7** directing the sharing of bread with the hungry, housing the homeless, and clothing the naked (cf. **Matthew 25:35–36**). Thus the Pharisees—like prosperity preachers today— severely miss, to their peril, the point of material blessing. It is not earthly reward for human righteousness to be squandered in unrighteousness; rather, it is earthly seed to be generously sown in humility for heavenly reward. In Ryle's words, "Wealth is not a sign of God's favor; poverty is not a sign of God's displeasure" (*Luke,* 215).

Not only did Jesus state unequivocally that hell is real, but also that there is an unbridgeable, uncrossable chasm between—"No traffic moves between heaven and hell" (Philips, 221). The fate of the two men ends with an "utter and unchangeable finality" (Craddock, 192). Death visits ten out of ten people and strikes both the poor and the rich—for one, the trials end; for the other, the blessings end—for both, judgment begins. "Death is a great fact that everyone acknowledges but very few people take into account," states Ryle (*Luke*, 215), adding, "There are perhaps few more awful passages in the Bible than this" (216).

III. A PLEA FOR THOSE STILL LIVING (Luke 16:27–31)

Jesus closed out this parable with the rich man making a final appeal to Abraham on behalf of those he left behind. Still arrogant, the rich man asked for Lazarus to be sent back among the living to warn his brothers of the torment to come if they do not make things right (i.e., repent). In both Jewish and Hellenistic traditions, there was a belief that the dead are able to make appeals on behalf of the living; this is why, in Catholic traditions, people pray to patron saints.

A Picture of a Final Plea (verses 27–31)

27 Then he said, I pray thee therefore, father, that thou wouldest send him to my father's house: 28 For I have five brethren; that he may testify unto them, lest they also come into this place of torment. 29 Abraham saith unto him, They have Moses and the prophets; let them hear them. 30 And he said, Nay, father Abraham: but if one went unto them from the dead, they will repent. 31 And he said unto him, If they hear not Moses and the prophets, neither will they be persuaded, though one rose from the dead.

According to Craddock, the Pharisees "did not follow their own scripture, the 'Law and the Prophets' (**verse 16**); so they were no better than the rich man's brothers who 'have Moses and the Prophets' (**verse 29**)" (*Luke*, 421). The rich man found out the hard way just how far off was his and his family's interpretation of scripture. Abraham informed him that the scriptures would be sufficient to teach his brothers properly if only they would be willing to listen. Speaking through Abraham to the Pharisees via the parable, Jesus exposed their flawed theology and their empty hearts.

The rich man desperately believed if his brothers only saw Lazarus alive, they would repent. Jesus clearly stated that not even a dead person raised to life would persuade the hard-hearted (**verse 31**). The Pharisees soon would personally witness this event twice, and their hearts not only would remain stone cold but would grow even more evil. Craddock writes: "The rejection of the risen Christ had its root in the misunderstanding of the true meaning of the Law and the Prophets" (*Luke*, 197). Everything Jesus did was true to scripture and, most importantly, according to a proper understanding of it—about which He was intentional in teaching His disciples (**24:25–27, 44–47**).

This parable contains a strong warning to heed the Word when it brings conviction and to not harden your heart, because your decisions in life have consequences on the inevitable judgment day. Stein said, "Life is to be lived with eternity's values in view" (*Luke,* 421). Jesus made it clear that that the rich man's eternal demise came from his own decisions and hardness of heart—just like the Pharisees consciously and selectively rejected the words of Moses and the prophets (**Luke 16:29;** cf. **John 5:46**). He may have prophesied about His own resurrection, knowing that not even that miracle of miracles would cause them to repent and change their ways.

Please note it was not the rich man's wealth that condemned him; it is not evil to be blessed with wealth. It was his lack of compassion that was his undoing. Like a rich fool, he had no eternal wealth and lost his soul to the deceitfulness of temporal wealth (cf. **Luke 12:21, 33, 16:11**).

SEARCH THE SCRIPTURES

QUESTION

How many brothers did the rich man have? **He had five brothers.**

BIBLE APPLICATION

AIM: Students will not allow selfishness to blind them to the need of others.

Even in our churches, we often measure people by what they do, what they have, and who they know rather than their display of Christ-like character. This is not the way of the kingdom. We live in a self-centered, entertainment-driven, over-stimulated world where we are raising a generation of young people who have no regard for the sacrifices made to enjoy the freedoms we have today.

In striving for a better life, we have forgotten it was in our struggle that we banded together as a people and that this is the very foundation of our dignity—the heart of compassion to look at each other as brother and sister. This lesson reminds us that God does not want us to shut our eyes, close our ears, and cover our mouths when we see social injustices. We have a mandate from God to care for the poor, disenfranchised, and marginalized. In the end, God will see to it that those who honor the poor honor Him and will be richly rewarded.

STUDENTS' RESPONSES

AIM: Students will be eager to seek out ways to meet the needs of others.

Pray and ask God how you can individually and corporately be an agent of change to provide for the poor. Begin to pray and intercede for those who have abundance to have a heart for God so that they come alongside to advance the kingdom through wise use of their resources. Seek out opportunities to be a blessing to someone in need and to not pass by someone on the street who is hungry or in need of clothes or shelter. As we give and share with the least of these, we do it as unto the Lord, and He is pleased. Examine how you can be proactive in helping to change the attitudes about the poor in your community and help young people to be sensitive to the needs of others. Go beyond your comfort zone to extend a helping hand.

PRAYER

Father, we praise you because you are a compassionate God. We thank you for showing us compassion and meeting our deepest need for a Savior. Lord, we ask that you would give us the same compassion that you have. We pray that you help us to be ready to help others and meet the needs of those around us. In Jesus' name we pray. Amen.

DIG A LITTLE DEEPER

This lesson poses a question that we should ask ourselves. What have I done with everything God has given me? What have I done in the words of the young people to "pay it forward"? God allows his compassion, His grace, and mercy toward us so that we may see the need when a "Lazarus" is in our midst. We cannot assume that someone else will meet the need of a brother or sister. God illustrates His love for the poor and He even expresses how He feels when they are neglected. We should not throw the crumbs from our tables and be satisfied with this as our Christian duty. It is understood that when the poor beggar died he immediately went into the presence of the Lord. Coincidently his name meant "God is Help". When the rich man died he lifted his eyes in hell. The rich man must have realized why he was in hell. He realized that there would not be another chance for him to show love or give to the poor so he wanted to send a message to his brothers. Perhaps that message was "For what will it profit a man if he gains the whole world and loses his soul? Or what shall a man give in return for his soul? (Matt 16:26) (KJV). Your name shall be called HELP.

HOW TO SAY IT

Lazarus. LA-za-rus, LAZ-rus.

Bosom. BU-zum.

PREPARE FOR NEXT SUNDAY

Read **James 1:19–27** and study "Hear and Do the Word."

COMMENTS / NOTES:

_____

_____

_____

DAILY HOME BIBLE READINGS

MONDAY
An Open Hand to the Poor
(Deuteronomy 15:7–11)

TUESDAY
The Cry of the Poor and Afflicted
(Job 34:17–30)

WEDNESDAY
False Concern for the Poor
(John 12:1–8)

THURSDAY
I Will Give to the Poor
(Luke 19:1–10)

FRIDAY
Shrewdness and the Future
(Luke 16:1–9)

SATURDAY
Master of the Heart
(Luke 16:10–18)

SUNDAY
Comfort and Agony
(Luke 16:19–31)

HEAR AND DO THE WORD

BIBLE BASIS: JAMES 1:19–27

BIBLE TRUTH: Obedience to the Word is essential to victorious living.

MEMORY VERSE: "But be ye doers of the word, and not hearers only, deceiving your own selves" (James 1:22, KJV).

LESSON AIM: By the end of the lesson, we will: REVIEW the relationship that is expressed in the Scripture between hearing and doing the Word; EXPRESS our feelings about hearing and doing God's Word; and DEVELOP practical strategies for acting in accordance with what the Word says.

BACKGROUND SCRIPTURES: 1 John 3:14-20 — Read and incorporate the insights gained from the Background Scriptures into your study of the lesson.

LESSON SCRIPTURE

JAMES 1:19–27, KJV

19 Wherefore, my beloved brethren, let every man be swift to hear, slow to speak, slow to wrath:

20 For the wrath of man worketh not the righteousness of God.

21 Wherefore lay apart all filthiness and superfluity of naughtiness, and receive with meekness the engrafted word, which is able to save your souls.

22 But be ye doers of the word, and not hearers only, deceiving your own selves.

23 For if any be a hearer of the word, and not a doer, he is like unto a man beholding his natural face in a glass:

24 For he beholdeth himself, and goeth his way, and straightway forgetteth what manner of man he was.

25 But whoso looketh into the perfect law of liberty, and continueth therein, he being not a forgetful hearer, but a doer of the work, this man shall be blessed in his deed.

26 If any man among you seem to be religious, and bridleth not his tongue, but deceiveth his own heart, this man's religion is vain.

27 Pure religion and undefiled before God and the Father is this, To visit the fatherless and widows in their affliction, and to keep himself unspotted from the world.

BIBLICAL DEFINITIONS

A. Wrath (James 1:19) *orge* (Gk.)— Anger as a state of mind, indignation as an outburst of that state of mind with the purpose of revenge.

B. Meekness (v. 21) *prautes* (Gk.)—A condition of the mind and heart that demonstrates gentleness not in weakness but in power. A virtue of strength and character.

LIFE NEED FOR TODAY'S LESSON

AIM: Students will learn to not talk about what will help others but instead take action to help others.

INTRODUCTION
James and His Letter

James, the half-brother of Jesus, was among the early leaders of the church and was based in Jerusalem. Although the epistle of James is placed toward the end of the New Testament, it is actually the first letter of instruction written to the church—thus the first book written. The primary audience for this epistle was Christian Jews spread across the world

due to persecution because of their faith in Christ.

The major theme of James' letter was to offer instruction for godly living in the midst of a self-indulgent world. This letter is viewed as a book of wisdom and instruction for Jewish believers. James appealed for his fellow believers to put outward actions with their inward faith. Scholars believe that James wrote this epistle in the mid 40s A.D. around the time of the council in Jerusalem. He was the first Apostle martyr of the church, executed in A.D. 62.

BIBLE LEARNING

AIM: Students will learn how the Word of God will guide us in our daily encounters.

I. BASIC WISDOM
(James 1:19–20)

In proverb fashion, James instructed believers to "be swift to hear, slow to speak, slow to wrath" (**verse 19**). This letter was written early in the church's life. The believers were facing persecution for their faith in Jesus Christ. As James offered up his instruction, he most likely used as basis from his own upbringing a combination of wisdom Scriptures such as **Proverbs 10:19, 4:17, 19**, and **Ecclesiastes 5:2**.

Wisdom literature was captured by scribes and passed down orally as Jews met in the synagogues and talked in their homes.

James reminded readers that anger does not produce the righteous living that God desires from His people (**James 1:20**). In the previous verses, he implored those who were lacking wisdom to ask God for it (**verses 5–6**); **Ecclesiastes 7:9** says, "Be not hasty in thy spirit to be angry: for anger resteth in the bosom of fools." It does not work in our favor or God's when we are unable to control our emotions. God is patient and longsuffering with us; therefore, we must do the same for others.

Behaving the Word (verses 19–20)
19 Wherefore, my beloved brethren, let every man be swift to hear, slow to speak, slow to wrath: 20 For the wrath of man worketh not the righteousness of God.

James began by acknowledging that the ones to whom he was writing were also children of God the Father and righteous Judge. Therefore, there existed a bond of love between Him and them. It is from that sense of love that James admonished the believers (both Jews scattered around the known world and Gentiles who had put their faith in Christ) to remember, to "hear" (Gk. *akouo*, a-KOO-o, meaning to attend to, consider what is or has been said) the Word of God that had already been entrusted to them so that they would not fall under His judgment. James knew that a zealot-like fervor for rebellion was sweeping throughout the region, and many were being influenced by its call for violence against Rome. He did not want those who followed Christ to be caught up in the hostility and anger in the same manner as those who did not belong to the risen Lord.

God's Word is powerful. It has the ability to change hearts and affect character, but it should not be shared hastily with others until its work in the hearer is evident. James also admonished believers to be slow to wrath (Gk. *orge*, **or-GAY**, meaning any violent emotion but especially anger), so that, by their lives and actions, they would demonstrate that a different message was at work in their hearts. James understood that man's anger inhibits the development of God's righteous work within him.

II. REMEMBERING WHO WE ARE (James 1:21–25)

James used an illustration in **verses 23-24** to further drive home his point of how one can engage in self-deception about righteous living. When a person looks in a mirror, he or she sees an image for a moment, but when away from the mirror, the image is forgotten. The Word of God is our mirror to remind us that without Christ, our image is out of focus. Only when we look in the mirror of the Word and see the righteousness of Christ are we reminded what we are supposed to look like. The Word of God reminds us that we are in Christ but still growing into the knowledge of Him— which requires us to be diligent in study, fervent in prayer, and quick to obey. James went on to say that those who look into the perfect law of liberty, which is freedom in Christ, will live by the Word and be blessed.

Living by the Word (verses 21–25)
21 Wherefore lay apart all filthiness and superfluity of naughtiness, and receive with meekness the engrafted word, which is able to save your souls. 22 But be ye doers of the word, and not hearers only, deceiving your own selves. 23 For if any be a hearer of the word, and not a doer, he is like unto a man beholding his natural face in a glass: 24 For he beholdeth himself, and goeth his way, and straightway forgetteth what manner of man he was. 25 But whoso looketh into the perfect law of liberty, and continueth therein, he being not a forgetful hearer, but a doer of the work, this man shall be blessed in his deed.

Evil flows from within us and expresses itself in our actions toward others. James instructed the believers to put off all "filthiness" (Gk. *rhuparia*, **hroo-par-EE-ah**, meaning to defile or dishonor) as though it were a dirty, useless garment. The work of righteousness would then begin to show itself and help to empower the believers to hold in check the "superfluity" (Gk. *perisseia*, pronounced **per-is SI-ah**, meaning the wickedness remaining over in a Christian from his state prior to conversion) of "naughtiness" (Gk. *kakia*, **kak-EE-ah**, meaning malignity, malice, ill will, desire to injure). Such a state can only be accomplished in believers when they welcome the Word of God with true humility.

James's admonition for believers, "be ye" (Gk. *gino mai*, **GHIN-om-ahee**, and carrying the implication to make sure that they are doers of the word), is to demonstrate to others how the Word of God is at work within them. They are to do this by the way they live before others and by making a habit of doing the Word. By offering the analogy of one looking at his face in a glass, James wants believers to reflect on the fact that the best mirrors of the day were made out of Corinthian brass but the image reflected back was often distorted. It would have been easy then for the individual to look at the reflection of his "natural" (Gk. *genesis*, **GHEN-es-is,** meaning that of his origin) face, turn away, and forget what he looked like or what he had become.

James contrasted the natural man with the spiritual man (see **John 3:6**). The Word of God, which produces the spiritual man, perfects the law and sets man free from his sinful nature or natural self. But in order for the Word of God to have its desired effect, believers need to "continueth" (Gk. *parameno,* **par-am-EN-o,** meaning to gaze or continue always near) in that Word. The act of gazing intently into the Word of God enables believers to retain the image of what the Holy Spirit is producing within them.

Dunn and Rogerson (*Commentary on the Bible,* 1486) suggest that in drawing the contrast between the individual who views his image in a glass and then forgets what he looks like and the individual who lingers or gazes at his reflection in the glass, James was making the same type of analogy that Jesus made in His story of the two men who built houses—one on the sand and the other on rock (**Matthew 7:24–27**). The blessing for the believer is founded upon the actions that flow from the changed life that is the product of the Holy Spirit's work. This blessing manifests itself in the deeds of the believer that are a result of having built inwardly upon the solid ground of the Word of God.

SEARCH THE SCRIPTURES

QUESTION

What does James say that believers should eradicate from their lives?

III. SELF-CONTROL AND PURITY (James 1:26–27)

It is not enough to give outward expressions of devotion to God when one's lifestyle does not reflect one's words. Attending church every Sunday, paying tithes, and serving in ministry should be done out of loving obedience to God and in gratitude for salvation through Jesus Christ, but it is all for naught if there is no true transformation of the heart. Our works should express our love and reverence and not be mere duty. Quoting Isaiah, Jesus said of the Pharisees, "This people draweth nigh unto me with their mouth, and honoreth me with their lips; but their heart is far from me. But in vain they do worship me, teaching for doctrines the commandments of men" (**Matthew 15:8–9**; cf. **Isaiah 29:13**).

Representing the Word (verses 26–27)

26 If any man among you seem to be religious, and bridleth not his tongue, but deceiveth his own heart, this man's religion is vain. 27 Pure religion and undefiled before God and the Father is this, To visit the fatherless and widows in their affliction, and to keep himself unspotted from the world.

For James, true religion is evidenced by the fruit that religion produces in the individual. A true believer, one who has permitted the Word of God to take root within, will not be like the zealots who made uncontrolled and impassioned speeches against Roman occupation. Instead, that person will "bridleth" (Gk. *chalingagogeo,* **khal in-ag-ogue-EH-o,** meaning to hold in check or restrain) his tongue. The word that James used for "religious" (Gk. *threskos,* **THRACE-kos**) refers to giving scrupulous attention to the details of worship. This would include being careful of one's actions and one's speech when involved in religious activities. However, if one does not control his tongue when not engaged in religious activities, then that individual is only deceiving his own "heart" (Gk. *kardia*, **kar-DEE-ah,** meaning the center and seat of spiritual life). For that individual, religion is in "vain" (Gk. *mataios*, **MAT ah-yos**), which means his religion is useless and of no purpose.

James closed his counsel by explaining to believers that the type of religion that pleases God is both "pure" (Gk. *katharos*, **kath-ar-OS,** meaning free from corrupt desire, sin, and guilt) and "undefiled" (Gk. *amiantos*, **am-EE-antos,** meaning free from that by which the nature of a thing is deformed and debased, or its force and vigor impaired). The evidence that one possesses a religion that merits God's favor is found through the actions of visiting the fatherless and widows in times of distress, actions that reflect the work of the Holy Spirit on one's character. By encouraging believers to show concern for widows and the fatherless, James was reminding them that their Heavenly Father identified Himself as the God of the fatherless and the widow (**Psalm 68:5**).

SEARCH THE SCRIPTURES

QUESTION

James states in **James 1:26** that if the tongue is not "bridleth," what happens to a believer's heart and faith?

BIBLE APPLICATION

AIM: Students will remember to apply Bible concepts to their everyday lives.

At one time or another we are all guilty of talking a good game when it comes to living according to godly principles, representing the best of Christ in our sphere of influence, being concerned about the world around us, and having great intentions on being more helpful to those in need. In today's lesson, James calls us to not just be hearers of the Word but also to carry it out in our everyday lives in word, thought, and deed. Oftentimes, we can get stuck because there is so much to be done; it can be an overwhelming task to change the world— let alone ourselves! When we embrace change in baby steps, taking one action at a time and doing it consistently, transformation takes place. Physics says that for every action there is a reaction; James teaches us to have a better reaction to the world around us.

STUDENTS' RESPONSES

AIM: Students will learn to make a conscious effort to assess habits, behaviors, and actions that do not line up with the Word of God.

Really listen for God's instruction through the preached Word and in your time of personal devotion and Bible study. Take time to be quiet before the Lord and write down what He is speaking to you about through the Holy Spirit. As you listen, take steps to move in God's direction. Make a conscious effort to assess habits, behaviors, and actions that do not line up with the Word of God. Repent, and ask the Holy Spirit to help you act differently. Be patient with yourself. Trust that God has heard you and that His Word will change your heart if you yield to His way.

PRAYER

Father, we thank You that Your Word is a lamp to our feet and a light for our path (**Psalm 119**). We thank You that we have the privilege of making Your Word a part of our everyday life. We pray that we would be doers and not just hearers. We ask that You would show us where we need to change our minds and our actions. In Jesus' Name we pray. Amen.

DIG A LITTLE DEEPER

If we think that never backing down when we speak is a sign of strength. A soft answer turns away wrath. God wants us to practice self-control. He gives us the ability to hear and obey which will produce the fruit of the Spirit. It is the word of God that James focuses on as we strive to overcome our tests and trials and the consequences that come from not listening and not doing. When we listen to people we should seek to UNDERSTAND before we can be understood. First, we must practice self-control; not take offense so easily. Secondly, we should learn how to react and act toward criticism. Thirdly we should choose our words more carefully with no more meddling in other men's matters and simply rule our spirit. When tribulation or trouble comes we can see with double vision; which will be the ability to see the enemy for who he is. Matthew in chapter six said, "the lamp of the body is the eye. If therefore your eye is good, your whole body will be full of light. But if your eye is bad, your whole body will be full of darkness". He also said, "If therefore the light that is in you is darkness, how great is that darkness!" If we persevere and seek God for wisdom to overcome we will possess the fruit of righteousness and not give place to sin.

HOW TO SAY IT

Superfluity. su-per-**FLU**-it-ee.

Undefiled. un-**DE**-filed.

PREPARE FOR NEXT SUNDAY

Read **James 2:1–13** and study "Treat Everyone Equally."

Sources:
Dunn, James D. G. and John W. Rogerson. *Commentary on the Bible.* Grand Rapids, MI: Wm. B. Eerdmans Publishing Company, 2003.
HarperCollins Study Bible (NRSV). New York: Harper Collins Publishers, 2006. 2052–2054.
Hebrew Greek Key Word Study Bible (KJV), 2nd ed. Chattanooga, TN: AMG Publishers, 1991. 1528, 1743, 1751.
Keener, Craig S. *The IVP Bible Background Commentary: New Testament.* Downers Grove, IL: IVP Academic, 1994.
Tasker, R. V. G. *The General Epistle of James: An Introduction and Commentary.* Grand Rapids, MI: Wm. B. Eerdmans Publishing Company, 1982.
Unger, Merrill. *Unger's Bible Handbook.* Chicago: Moody Press, 1967. 785–786.

DAILY HOME BIBLE READINGS

MONDAY
A People Who Will Not Listen
(Jeremiah 7:21–28)

TUESDAY
A Lamp to Lighten My Darkness
(2 Samuel 22:26–31)

WEDNESDAY
The Voice of the Living God
(Deuteronomy 5:22–27)

THURSDAY
Neither Add nor Take Away Anything
(Deuteronomy 4:1–10)

FRIDAY
Denying God by Actions
(Titus 1:10–16)

SATURDAY
Love in Truth and Action
(1 John 3:14–20)

SUNDAY
Hearers and Doers of the Word
(James 1:19-27)

TREAT EVERYONE EQUALLY

BIBLE BASIS: JAMES 2:1–13

BIBLE TRUTH: Do not show favoritism.

MEMORY VERSE: "Hearken, my beloved brethren, Hath not God chosen the poor of this world rich in faith, and heirs of the kingdom which he hath promised to them that love him?" (James 2:5, KJV).

LESSON AIM: By the end of the lesson, we will: REVIEW James's writings concerning partiality and ways to avoid it; EXPLORE the full meaning of the phrase "Love your neighbor as yourself"; and INVESTIGATE ways we might discriminate against certain groups and find methods to instead demonstrate the love of God to those groups.

BACKGROUND SCRIPTURES: Romans 13:8-14 — Read and incorporate the insights gained from the Background Scriptures into your study of the lesson. Scriptures into your study of the lesson.

LESSON SCRIPTURE

JAMES 2:1 –13, KJV

1 My brethren, have not the faith of our Lord Jesus Christ, the Lord of glory, with respect of persons.

2 For if there come unto your assembly a man with a gold ring, in goodly apparel, and there come in also a poor man in vile raiment;

3 And ye have respect to him that weareth the gay clothing, and say unto him, Sit thou here in a good place; and say to the poor, Stand thou there, or sit here under my footstool:

4 Are ye not then partial in yourselves, and are become judges of evil thoughts?

5 Hearken, my beloved brethren, Hath not God chosen the poor of this world rich in faith, and heirs of the kingdom which he hath promised to them that love him?

6 But ye have despised the poor. Do not rich men oppress you, and draw you before the judgment seats?

7 Do not they blaspheme that worthy name by the which ye are called?

8 If ye fulfil the royal law according to the scripture, Thou shalt love thy neighbour as thyself, ye do well:

9 But if ye have respect to persons, ye commit sin, and are convinced of the law as transgressors.

10 For whosoever shall keep the whole law, and yet offend in one point, he is guilty of all.

11 For he that said, Do not commit adultery, said also, Do not kill. Now if thou commit no adultery, yet if thou kill, thou art become a transgressor of the law.

12 So speak ye, and so do, as they that shall be judged by the law of liberty.

13 For he shall have judgment without mercy, that hath shewed no mercy; and mercy rejoiceth against judgment.

BIBLICAL DEFINITIONS

A. Respect [of person] (James 2:1)
prosopolempsia (Gk.)—Partiality.

B. Blaspheme (v. 7) *blaspemeo*
(Gk.)—to speak reproachfully, rail at, revile, calumniate.

LIFE NEED FOR TODAY'S LESSON

AIM: Students will learn to treat everyone equally.

INTRODUCTION

Examples in James

The epistle of James is a letter written by James to remind those who had become prosperous about their foundations in the faith. The prosperous believers were identified by James as having "faith in our glorious Lord Jesus Christ" (from **James 2:1**, NLT). James used some examples from daily life to remind them of the commitment of faith they had made to Jesus Christ. James used himself as an example by first identifying himself as "a servant of God and of the Lord Jesus Christ" (from **1:1**). James chose two illustrations to demonstrate how partiality and ill treatment of the poor become stumbling blocks to believers and can contradict our faith in Jesus Christ.

BIBLE LEARNING

AIM: Students will learn not to show favoritism but to love one's neighbor as he or she would love oneself.

I. No favoritism among people (James 2:1–7)

James, who has been identified as the half-brother of Jesus Christ, wrote a letter of practicality to the believers. In this section, James addressed the moral behavior of believers toward the rich and the poor. James had just informed his readers what pure religion was all about. It was about serving those who are less fortunate— the orphans and the widows (**James 1:27**). Now it was time for him to look at some situations where professing Christians might not actually live out the faith in practice, and he begins here with the rich and the poor.

Practicing Faith in Personal Relationships (verses 1–7)

1 My brethren, have not the faith of our Lord Jesus Christ, the Lord of glory, with respect of persons. 2 For if there come unto your assembly a man with a gold ring, in goodly apparel, and there come in also a poor man in vile raiment; 3 And ye have respect to him that weareth the gay clothing, and say unto him, Sit thou here in a good place; and say to the poor, Stand thou there, or sit here under my footstool: 4 Are ye not then partial in yourselves, and are become judges of evil thoughts? 5 Hearken, my beloved brethren, Hath not God chosen the poor of this world rich in faith, and heirs of the kingdom which he hath promised to them that love him? 6 But ye have despised the poor. Do not rich men oppress you, and draw you before the judgment seats? 7 Do not they blaspheme that worthy name by the which ye are called?

Here James continued his admonitions from chapter 1 by instructing believers that they are to emulate the Lord Jesus Christ with regards to how they treat and view other people. Like Paul's admonition to the Romans to "be not conformed to this world" (**Romans 12:2**), James was trying to help believers understand that they were no longer to have the world's attitudes. They, as followers of Christ, were not to show personal favoritism.

James then gave an example of how believers might actually be showing favoritism toward people without even realizing it. By pointing at them "having respect" (Gk. *epiblepo,* **ep-ee-BLEP-o**) for the rich man over the poor man, James was drawing upon a common practice in the temples and courts of his society. In ancient Rome, the wearing of gold rings and fine robes spoke to membership in an elite class that always received favored treatment in Roman courts. Under Roman law, the poor could not bring accusations against people of higher class, and the penalties were often much harsher for the poor. Since the synagogue had become the place that served both as the house of prayer and as the community court, some of this same kind of favoritism was creeping in there as well. James counseled the believers against adopting such ways. The practice of showing such favoritism was strictly forbidden in Jewish law (cf. **Leviticus 19:13**), and it was contrary to the ideals established by the Lord Jesus Christ.

There is a sense of bewilderment in James' voice as he asked believers how they could be guilty of despising the poor in the same fashion that the rich did. It was the rich who oppressed *them*. It was the rich who dragged *them* into court. James's hearers were well aware of the fact that the wealthy classes were most guilty of oppressing Christians by dragging them before the court authorities for punishment (see **Acts 4:1–3** and **13:50** as examples). By "despising" (Gk. *atimato,* **at-im-AD-zo,** meaning to treat with contempt) the poor believers, they were showing by their actions that they had not really heard the Word of God. They were behaving just like the unsaved world around them, and that was unacceptable. God had chosen the "poor" (Gk. *ptochos,* **pto-KHOS,** meaning helpless, powerless to accomplish an end) to inherit His Kingdom and to be rich in "faith" (Gk. *pistis,* **PIS-tis,** meaning a strong and welcome conviction or belief that Jesus is the Messiah). James then reminded his hearers that the godless people they were emulating were the same ones who "blaspheme" (Gk. *blasphemeo,* **blas-fay-MEH-o**, meaning to speak reproachfully of, rail at, or revile) the name of the very Lord to whom they had given themselves. James chose the phrase "worthy name" to refer to Christ because it was uncommon to use the name of God; other forms of expression were found. In choosing the phrase "worthy name" (Gk. *kalos,* **kal-OS,** meaning beautiful by reason of purity of heart and life, and hence praiseworthy), James reminded his listeners that they now belonged to Christ and should embrace his example with regard to how they lived and functioned in the world.

SEARCH THE SCRIPTURES

QUESTION

How does James challenge believers

about their thoughts and ways about the poor?

I. NO FAVORITISM AMONG THE LAWS (James 2:8–13)

Here, James reminded the believers of Jesus' proclamation that the Kingdom of Heaven belongs to the poor. God will judge the believers on their treatment of the poor, especially if that treatment contradicts their faith statement. The believers were not showing love; instead, their behavior toward the poor was judgmental and would end in the believers themselves being judged by Jesus Christ: "So whatever you say or whatever you do, remember that you will be judged by the law that sets you free" (**verse 12, NLT**).

Practicing Faith in Interpersonal Relationships (verses 8–13)

8 If ye fulfill the royal law according to the scripture, Thou shalt love thy neighbor as thyself, ye do well. 9 But if ye have respect to persons, ye commit sin, and are convinced of the law as transgressors. 10 For whosoever shall keep the whole law, and yet offend in one point, he is guilty of all. 11 For he that said, Do not commit adultery, said also, Do not kill. Now if thou commit no adultery, yet if thou kill, thou art become a transgressor of the law. 12 So speak ye, and so do, as they that shall be judged by the law of liberty. 13 For he shall have judgment without mercy, that hath shewed no mercy; and mercy rejoiceth against judgment.

When Christ was asked to identify the greatest commandment, He told His listeners that they needed to love. First, they were to love God with all their hearts, souls, and minds, and then they were to love their neighbors in the same ways that they loved themselves (see **Matthew 22:37–40**). James called this the "royal" law because it was universally held in Jewish society that God's laws were higher than judicial laws; this law was a direct decree from God (see **Leviticus 19:18**) and was to be regarded as the highest, a law given by the King of kings Himself. The "neighbor" (Gk. *plesion*, **play-SEE-on**, meaning friend) to whom James was referring was anyone in need.

The Jewish society of James' day viewed a neighbor only as a fellow Jew. But James was seeking to guide his listeners into an understanding that their view of what made one a neighbor had to be expanded. Anyone bearing the name of Christ and belonging to His Kingdom was now to be included. Failure to follow the royal law would bring the "transgressor" (Gk. *parabates*, **par-ab-AT ace**, meaning one who breaks God's law) under God's penalty.

James drove home the point that the smallest transgression of God's law makes one guilty of violating the whole law. A chain with a broken link is just a broken chain or a piece of clothing that has a tear in it is just a damaged piece of clothing. James was trying to help his listeners understand that they were not to pick and choose when it comes to obeying God's commands. By choosing the imagery of someone who would not commit adultery but would kill, James might have had in mind the zealots who were so pious that they would never commit adultery but who also had no compunction about assassinating those they deemed worthy of death. God is not honored when we follow some of His commands and not others because we find some more acceptable than others.

Finally, James cautioned his listeners to "speak" (Gk. *laleo,* **lal-EH-o,** meaning to use words in order to declare one's mind and disclose one's thoughts) and to "do" (Gk. *poieo,* **poy-EH-o,** meaning to carry out, to execute) as those who would be judged by the law of liberty, which was the standard that was set by the Lord Jesus Christ (see **1:25**). James was again reminding believers that because they had taken Christ into themselves, the Spirit of Christ was at work transforming their nature into something that was pleasing and acceptable to a holy God. This transformation should show itself in their speech and actions.

Jewish teachers often defined God's character by two attributes: mercy and justice. Mercy meant to show kindness or goodwill toward others, while justice meant condemnation. Both belong to the providence of God. James stated the truth that God's mercy will be shown to those who themselves show mercy, and God's condemnation will fall on anyone who does not show mercy. Believers who show kindness and goodwill toward others, then, need never fear being on the receiving end of God's judgment because Jesus has declared that the merciful will receive God's mercy (see **Matthew 5:7**).

SEARCH THE SCRIPTURES

QUESTION

Believers, according to James, commit sin when this happens.

BIBLE APPLICATION

AIM: Students will understand that the solution to all the world's problems is found in the word "love."

Love will conquer society's question of marriage. Love will decrease the murder rate. Love will stifle greed. Love will conquer racism and sexism. Love will conquer addictions. Love will end believers' segregated worship hour. Love will encourage doers of the Word. Love's motto will be, "Thy will be done" (**Matthew 26:42**).

STUDENTS' RESPONSES

AIM: Students will learn to be an example of the love of God.

An active example of God's love is to initiate inter faith worship with a church of another ethnicity. Regularly commit to regular fellowship with one another. Encourage the study of God's Word together. Begin conversations on how the dynamics of the Bible sustain each group. Evangelize together to demonstrate that we are "all one in Christ Jesus" (**Galatians 3:28**).

PRAYER

Father, we know that You created all people as brothers and sisters. We know that Your love welcomes all and that You show no favoritism. Lord, we ask that You would use us as Your instruments to love every one regardless of their race or social status. We pray that You would use us to welcome them into Your Kingdom.

In Jesus' Name we pray. Amen.

DIG A LITTLE DEEPER

God wants us to be able to do the same things for everybody. He does not discriminate. Equal does not mean that we are all the same. Each of us is different in our special way but we also have the common qualities that make us all human. We should be treated with respect and dignity and treat others in the same way.

James here focuses on us showing favoritism to someone because of social class, wealth, and all other actions. It is natural for the world to honor those who are of a higher class; Hollywood and all the movie stars, politicians, etc. are chosen favorites but as Christians, we should have a different set of values. We should esteem individuals for different reasons than the world does. Even the poor man should have a place to sit. Moses reminded the people in Deuteronomy. 1:17 that we should not respect persons in judgment; but we should hear the small as well as the great. "Ye shall not be afraid of the face of man; for the judgment is God's." Whether we are wearing a gold ring and fine clothes or a poor man in filthy old clothes ALL should be invited to the feast.

HOW TO SAY IT

Raiment. **RAY**-ment.

Transgressors. trans-**gres**-ors.

PREPARE FOR NEXT SUNDAY

Read **James 2:14–26** and study "Show Your Faith By Your Works."

Sources:

Draper, Charles W., Chad Brand, and Archie England, eds. *Holman Illustrated Bible Dictionary.* Grand Rapids, MI: Holman Reference, 2003.

Dunn, James D. G. and John W. Rogerson. *Commentary on the Bible.* Grand Rapids, MI: Wm. B. Eerdmans Publishing Company: 2003.

Keener, Craig S. *The IVP Bible Background Commentary: New Testament.* Downers Grove, IL: IVP Academic, 1994.

Myers, Allen C., John W. Simpson, Philip A. Frank, Timothy P. Jenney, and Ralph W. Vunderink, eds. *The Eerdmans Bible Dictionary.* Grand Rapids, MI: Wm. B. Eerdmans Publishing Company, 1996.

Radmacher, Earl D., Ronald B. Allen, and H. W. House, eds. *Nelson Study Bible* (NKJV). Nashville: Thomas Nelson Publishers, 2001.

Tasker, R. V. G. *The General Epistle of James: An Introduction and Commentary.* Grand Rapids, MI: Wm. B. Eerdmans Publishing Company, 1982.

Today's Parallel Bible (KJV/NIV/NASB/NLT). Grand Rapids, MI: Zondervan, 2000.

DAILY HOME BIBLE READINGS

MONDAY
Judging Rightly and Impartially
(Deuteronomy 1:9–18)

TUESDAY
Judging on the Lord's Behalf
(2 Chronicles 19:1–7)

WEDNESDAY
Giving Justice to the Weak
(Psalm 82)

THURSDAY
Showing Partiality is Not Good
(Proverbs 28:18–22)

FRIDAY
God Shows No Partiality
(Acts 10:34–43)

SATURDAY
Put on the Lord Jesus Christ
(Romans 13:8–14)

SUNDAY
Faith and Favoritism
(James 2:1–13)

SHOW YOUR FAITH BY YOUR WORKS

BIBLE BASIS: JAMES 2:14–26

BIBLE TRUTH: Practice what you believe.

MEMORY VERSE: "For as the body without the spirit is dead, so faith without works is dead also" (James 2:26, KJV).

LESSON AIM: By the end of the lesson, we will: REVIEW the connection James makes between faith and works; EXPRESS what it means to declare one's faith by performing good works; and CONSIDER a faith statement and identify how it may manifest itself through works.

BACKGROUND SCRIPTURES: Luke 7:1-10 — Read and incorporate the insights gained from the Background Scriptures into your study of the lesson.

LESSON SCRIPTURE

JAMES 2:14 –26, KJV

14 What doth it profit, my brethren, though a man say he hath faith, and have not works? can faith save him?

15 If a brother or sister be naked, and destitute of daily food,

16 And one of you say unto them, Depart in peace, be ye warmed and filled; notwithstanding ye give them not those things which are needful to the body; what doth it profit?

17 Even so faith, if it hath not works, is dead, being alone.

18 Yea, a man may say, Thou hast faith, and I have works: shew me thy faith without thy works, and I will shew thee my faith by my works.

19 Thou believest that there is one God; thou doest well: the devils also believe, and tremble.

20 But wilt thou know, O vain man, that faith without works is dead?

21 Was not Abraham our father justified by works, when he had offered Isaac his son upon the altar?

22 Seest thou how faith wrought with his works, and by works was faith made perfect?

23 And the scripture was fulfilled which saith, Abraham believed God, and it was imputed unto him for righteousness: and he was called the Friend of God.

24 Ye see then how that by works a man is justified, and not by faith only.

25 Likewise also was not Rahab the harlot justified by works, when she had received the messengers, and had sent them out another way?

26 For as the body without the spirit is dead, so faith without works is dead also.

BIBLICAL DEFINITIONS

A. Faith (James 2:14) *pistis* (Gk.)— Belief and trust in God.

B. Works (v. 14) *ergon* (Gk.)—Behavior, actions. Works are character traits of faith.

LIFE NEED FOR TODAY'S LESSON

AIM: That your students would show evidence of their faith not just in actions and not just words.

INTRODUCTION

A Faithful Lifestyle

This is a continuation of James' letter to the believers on why the actual practice of one's faith in day-to-day living is more important than one's statement of faith. With the completion of teaching on the practice of faith, James shifted to the underlying principles of faith's lifestyle— the attitude of faith followed by actions of faith. James clearly states, "Faith by itself isn't enough. Unless it produces good deeds, it is dead and useless" (from James 2:17, NLT).

BIBLE LEARNING

AIM: Students will learn about the relationship between works and faith.

I. BENEFITING THE FAITH
(James 2:14–17)

The authenticity of one's faith is determined by its usefulness. "Usefulness," as defined by the American Heritage Dictionary, is having a "beneficial use." A beneficial use for the believer is a statement of faith followed by actions of faith. The role model for the believer to emulate is Jesus Christ. "For even the Son of Man came not to be served but to serve others and to give his life as a ransom for many" (Matthew 20:28, NLT).

Usefulness of One's Faith
(verses 14–17)
14 What doth it profit, my brethren, though a man say he hath faith, and have not works? can faith save him?

15 If a brother or sister be naked, and destitute of daily food, 16 And one of you say unto them, Depart in peace, be ye warmed and filled; notwithstanding ye give them not those things which are needful to the body; what doth it profit? 17 Even so faith, if it hath not works, is dead, being alone.

It may be helpful to note that the literary construction of this part of James is one of a proposition supported by arguments and then summarized with conclusions. The proposition opens with a pair of rhetorical questions, the first of which basically says, "Suppose a man says he has faith." This is quite different from James wording it, "Suppose

a man has faith." To actually have faith versus saying you have faith are two entirely different things. The second rhetorical question today would be worded, "This kind of faith—claimed faith without works—can't save him, can it?" Of course, the correct answer is no, as James will demonstrate.

The proposition continues with a hypothetical example, employing hyperbole with a "naked" brother or sister (Gk. *gymno* , gum-NOS), indicating someone in dire straits or desperate need, reinforced with the supporting phrase "destitute of daily food." The common phrase "Depart in peace" means, in essence, "Go get what you need somewhere else, from someone else—but know that I care," or the popular "Go and be filled." Such words come from a faith that is useless and dead (Gk. *nekros* , ne-KROS), which is the plain sense of the word; James was not pulling punches. "What good is a faith like that?" James asked. In other words, what good is a dead faith? Burdick writes, as if to respond, "Its

73

sccming concern for the welfare of the poor is a worthless façade" (Hebrews, James,1, 2 Peter 1, 2, 3 John, Jude, Revelation, 183).

Salvation or justification, it can be said, is comprised of both hearing and doing; the same can be said of faith and works (cf. Matthew 7:24; 1 Thessalonians 1:3). The same is not true of the inverse, as if it were a formula, that hearing plus doing results in salvation, or that faith plus works results in the same (cf. Romans 10:9; James 1:23, 25, 2:14, 24). Just because something is true doesn't automatically mean the inverse is also true; that is, the fact that some roses are red does not also mean that red is only seen on some roses. Rather, genuine faith is a gift that comes from God (Ephesians 2:8) and works are a natural expression of such faith. Per Burdick, "Action is the proper fruit of living faith" (Hebrews, James, 1, 2 Peter, 1, 2, 3 John, Jude, Revelation, 182). Faith and works are two sides of the same coin.

For many, Paul and James have put faith and works at odds—and too often the argument has been framed as if one must make an either/or choice. Kistemaker writes, "To put the matter in different words, James explains the active side of faith and Paul the passive side" (James and I–III John, 87). In reality, they were talking about two types of faith— only one of which is alive, while the other is dead, incapable of saving anyone (cf. Galatians 5:6, 6:15; 1 Corinthians 7:19).

SEARCH THE SCRIPTURES

QUESTION

James states what about faith?

II . DEAD FAITH (James 2:18–20)

But the declarant makes a key mistake in the text: He wants to assert the divisibility of one's faith and works. For James, the two can't be divided, which makes the following easier to digest: "Now someone may argue, 'Some people have faith; others have good deeds.' But I say, 'How can you show me your faith if you don't have good deeds? I will show you my faith by my good deeds'" (James 2:18 , NLT).

Faith Without Works is Dead (verses 18–20)

18 Yea, a man may say, Thou hast faith, and I have works: shew me thy faith without thy works, and I will shew thee my faith by my works. 19 Thou believest that there is one God; thou doest well: the devils also believe, and tremble. 20 But wilt thou know, O vain man, that faith without works is dead?

Having stated his proposition with rhetorical and hypothetical questions that beg an obvious answer, James next argued his case via a fictional debater. Person A has faith without deeds; Person B has faith with deeds. From Person A, James asked for evidence of the faith he claimed to possess, reminding him that even demons can make such claims. For Person B, the evidence of faith speaks for itself—the deeds are the evidence. In Burdick's words, "This epistle leaves no place for a religion that is mere mental acceptance of truth" (Hebrews,James, 1, 2 Peter, 1, 2, 3 John, Jude, Revelation , 182).

III . TESTED FAITH (James 2:21–26)

It isn't enough to hold right doctrine or truth, especially when it is not lived out practically. Abraham could have believed

God was sovereign, but neglecting to obey when called to sacrifice his son would have told a different story. Instead, his actions supported his belief. Many Christians need to properly understand what James is getting at here. Living a life submitted to God isn't just about following rules and regulations; it's about living out your faith daily through your deeds. We can believe that the Christian life is about practicing patience toward others, but what happens when our patience is tested? It is through these tests that we move closer and closer to what James calls "perfect and complete, wanting nothing" (James 1:4).

Acts of Faith (verses 21–26)

21 Was not Abraham our father justified by works, when he had offered Isaac his son upon the altar? 22 Seest thou how faith wrought with his works, and by works was faith made perfect? 23 And the scripture was fulfilled which saith, Abraham believed God, and it was imputed unto him for righteousness: and he was called the Friend of God. 24 Ye see then how that by works a man is justified, and not by faith only. 25 Likewise also was not Rahab the harlot justified by works, when she had received the messengers, and had sent them out another way? 26 For as the body without the spirit is dead, so faith without works is dead also.

It would be both normal and expected for any Jew talking about faith to mention Abraham. Both Paul (Romans 4:9) and James describe God calling Abraham righteous because of his faith. James here revisited the familiar details of Abraham's "works"—offering Isaac on the altar by faith— actively trusting God. Per Kistemaker, "Faith and action, then, are never separated. The one flows

naturally from the other" (James and I–III John , 98).

James was saying that Abraham's obedient "work"—a tangible act of faith in putting Isaac on the altar and being willing to sacrifice even the sonof promise at God's command— was a fulfillment of Scripture. James referred to Genesis 15:6 (see also 2 Chronicles 20:7) when God reckoned as righteous Abraham's faith in the seemingly impossible covenant promise of countless generations born to an elderly couple. Abraham had faith, and Godmade a covenant with him because of it. Then Abraham proved his faith with the "work" of obeying God and being willing to sacrifice Isaac.

James next appealed to an opposite type of character from the Old Testament for "Exhibit B" of the argument part of his presentation. Some might feel as if they cannot relate to the head of the Jewish nation, the national shining star, Abraham. What about an example from the opposite side of society— would that be closer to home or at least more relatable? From Kistemaker, "Abraham demonstrated both faith and works, but so did Rahab— and she was a prostitute" (James and I–III John, 99).

This unlikely pair shared both differences and similarities. One was Hebrew, the other Gentile; one was called by God, the other originally destined for destruction; one was a man, the other a woman; one was the father of faith, the other a lowly prostitute; one went through a long-term process of interacting with God and proving his faith; the other only had hearsay to guide her quick thinking. For similarities, both were foreigners, both showed hospitality to strangers (Genesis 18:1–5; Joshua 2:1), and both became ancestors of Jesus (Matthew

1:2, 5). Rahab took her place in history next to Abraham because she had faith in God and acted on her faith—a simple but profound lesson that is completely transcultural for all believers.

James made his second parallel conclusion, creating a second passage that many after him will neatly clip from its clear context and use to make claims that do not square with either his complete argument or the whole counsel of God from both testaments. From Kistemaker, "What we have in this comparison [between Abraham and Rahab] is not a contrast of faith over against works. The point is that faith by itself is dead, much the same as the body withoutthe spirit is dead" (James and I–III John, 101).

The concept of faith without works is so easy that even demons can do it. No lifestyle change is needed nor are sacrifices required. No compassion is necessary and no giving of time, treasure, or talent will be expected. Most Americans claim to be "Christian," but how many live Christian lives? Many attend church occasionally, or regularly, but what are they doing during the week?

How much faith is being exercised for the millions who are "C. E." Christians—darkening the doorways of churches only on Christmas and Easter? A modern adage holds that standing in a donut shop doesn't make one a donut, and walking into a garage doesn't turn someone into a car. Perhaps Christians would do well to cease and desist from justifying their absence or lack of compassion and instead begin at once to incarnate the hands and feet and heart of Jesus in a cold, lonely, and desperate world. From Kistemaker, "Religion that is spiritual ministers to the need that is physical"

(James and I–III John, 102).

SEARCH THE SCRIPTURES QUESTION

Abraham is noted by James as being called what in relationship to God because of his faith and actions?

BIBLE APPLICATION

AIM: Students will understand that they need to do more than only make a statement of faith.

In today's society, with its increasing hostility toward Christians, believers need to do more than make a statement of faith. As followers of Jesus, believers need to put their statement of faith into action to display and represent God's love for all mankind. With an increasing disparity between the "haves and have nots," it is important now more than ever for believers to address the needs of the have nots and speak words of encouragement, hope, and love.

STUDENTS' RESPONSES

AIM: Students will keep their faith alive by their works.

The mind-set of the believer must first be to serve. Some suggestions for serving are making regular visits with shut-ins, getting involved in a ministry that provides physical food and spiritual food, or perhaps creating a job training center (based on talent within one's congregation) that can address the needs of young people who lack their GED and need relevant job training.

PRAYER

Father, we thank You that Your presence in our lives is not just mere words. We thank You for showing up in power and being active in our situations. Father, we pray that You would help us to keep our faith alive and dynamic through works. We pray that we would not just give lip service to Your Word, but that we would serve You from our hearts and in our actions. In Jesus' Name we pray.

Amen.

DIG A LITTLE DEEPER

The fruit of a born-again believer is a transformed life. What good is driving a car without an ignition switch? You must believe that it will start but there must be a key. If we claim to have faith we must have the evidence or key. Our evidence shows and our faith grows when we take action. Salvation is proving to anyone that your confession is authentic by the life you live. For James it was perseverance, purity, being impartial, truthful, patient, and having compassion for people in need. If our faith does not consist of these things then our works are dead. This specifically includes true compassion for those who need clothes, food, and shelter. James wants us to realize that our faith must not just be confessed but professed by what we do to bring Him glory.

HOW TO SAY IT

Destitute. **DES**-te-toot.

Imputed. im-**PYUT**-ed.

Rahab. **RAY**-hab.

PREPARE FOR NEXT SUNDAY

Read James 3:1–12 and study "Control Your Speech."

Sources:
Blue Letter Bible. BlueLetterBible.org. http://www.blueletterbible.org/ (accessed Monday, December 17, 2011).
Burdick, Donald W. "James." The Expositor's Bible Commentary with the

New International Version: Hebrews, James, 1, 2 Peter, 1, 2, 3 John, Jude, Revelation, Vol. 12. Edited by Frank E. Gaebelein. Grand Rapids, MI: Zondervan, 1981. 181–185.
Draper, Charles W., Chad Brand, and Archie England, eds. Holman Illustrated Bible Dictionary. Grand Rapids, MI: Holman Reference, 2003.
Kistemaker, Simon J. James and I–III John. New Testament Commentary. Grand Rapids, MI: Baker Publishing Group, 1986. 87–102.
Martin, R. A. and John H. Elliott. James, 1–2 Peter, Jude. Augsburg Commentary on the New Testament. Minneapolis: Fortress Press, 1982. 28–36.
Myers, Allen C., John W. Simpson, Philip A. Frank, Timothy P. Jenney, and Ralph W. Vunderink, eds. The Eerdmans Bible Dictionary. Grand Rapids, MI: Wm. B. Eerdmans Publishing Company, 1996.
Radmacher, Earl D., Ronald B. Allen, and H. W. House, eds. Nelson Study Bible (NKJV). Nashville: Thomas Nelson Publishers, 2001.
Today's Parallel Bible (KJV/NIV/NASB/NLT). Grand Rapids, MI: Zondervan, 2000.

DAILY HOME BIBLE READINGS

MONDAY
The Work of Faith with Power
(2 Thessalonians 1:3–12)

TUESDAY
Faith Distracted by Loving Money
(1 Timothy 6:6–12)

WEDNESDAY
Completing What's Lacking in Faith
(1 Thessalonians 3:4–13)

THURSDAY
An Example of Great Faith
(Luke 7:1–10)

FRIDAY
A Faith that Saves
(Luke 7:36–50)

SATURDAY
Living Your Life in Christ
(Colossians 2:1–7)

SUNDAY
Faith Demonstrated through Works
(James 2:14–26)

CONTROL YOUR SPEECH

BIBLE BASIS: JAMES 3:1–12

BIBLE TRUTH: It is important to study the impact of words on others.

MEMORY VERSE: "Out of the same mouth proceedeth blessing and cursing. My brethren, these things ought not so to be" (James 3:10, KJV).

LESSON AIM: By the end of the lesson, we will: REVIEW James's teachings concerning how we speak to others; EXPRESS how it feels to be criticized and praised; and FIND WAYS to express praise and criticism in love despite the circumstances.

BACKGROUND SCRIPTURES: Proverbs 18:2-13 — Read and incorporate the insights gained from the Background Scriptures into your study of the lesson.

LESSON SCRIPTURE

JAMES 3:1–12, KJV

1 My brethren, be not many masters, knowing that we shall receive the greater condemnation.

2 For in many things we offend all. If any man offend not in word, the same is a perfect man, and able also to bridle the whole body.

3 Behold, we put bits in the horses' mouths, that they may obey us; and we turn about their whole body. 4 Behold also the ships, which though they be so great, and are driven of fierce winds, yet are they turned about with a very small helm, whithersoever the governor listeth.

5 Even so the tongue is a little member, and boasteth great things. Behold, how great a matter a little fire kindleth!

6 And the tongue is a fire, a world of iniquity: so is the tongue among our members, that it defileth the whole body, and setteth on fire the course of nature; and it is set on fire of hell.

7 For every kind of beasts, and of birds, and of serpents, and of things in the sea, is tamed, and hath been tamed of mankind:

8 But the tongue can no man tame; it is an unruly evil, full of deadly poison.

9 Therewith bless we God, even the Father; and therewith curse we men, which are made after the similitude of God.

10 Out of the same mouth proceedeth blessing and cursing. My brethren, these things ought not so to be.

11 Doth a fountain send forth at the same place sweet water and bitter?

12 Can the fig tree, my bretren, bear olive berries? either a vine, figs? so can no fountain both yield salt water and fresh.

BIBLICAL DEFINITIONS

A. We offend (James 3:2) *ptaio* (Gk.)— To cause someone to fall or stumble.

B. Boasteth great things (v. 5) *aucheo* (Gk.)—Haughty language that wounds.

LIFE NEED FOR TODAY'S LESSON

AIM: Sudents will make sure their words will benefit others who hear them.

INTRODUCTION

Apostolic Guidance

During the time of this writing, religious leaders were no longer ignoring the new Christian church. Although they were still a part of Judaism, Christians were now being singled out, and the persecution of Christians had begun in earnest. Two other men named James mentioned in the New Testament (the Apostle identified as the son of Zebedee and the brother of John; and the Apostle identified as the son of Alphaeus) had been martyred. Similarly, Stephen had been stoned to death for his faith. In this increasingly hostile and dangerous atmosphere, it is not surprising that many Christians were abandoning the faith.

Internal strife was also taking place within the church. Christians were dealing with doctrinal arguments, false teachers, power struggles, gossip, and slander. The Christians were being encouraged to pursue self-fulfillment. During this time, many philosophers believed and taught the importance of knowledge for the sake of knowledge. Very little importance was placed on putting knowledge into practice. They mistakenly taught that the way to spiritual enlightenment was through knowledge. James wrote to combat this mind-set. Faith, not knowledge, is key. Our faith is rooted in our hearts; it is this faith that transforms us into "doers." Man, James insisted, must seek to attain the will of God. Only then can he bring about a change in his life and in the life of the church.

BIBLE LEARNING

AIM: Students will learn the importance of self discipline in their speech.

I. A TEACHING TONGUE
(James 3:1–4)

In James 1 and 2, we are taught that Christians can be identified by the attitude they maintain during their suffering and by their obedience to God's will and His way. James next turned his attention to Christian speech. During James' time, rabbis and teachers abounded. All of them claimed to know the "truth." James understood that many of these men taught because of the esteem it brought them, not because they were called to teach. They viewed it as an occupation, not as a service to God. James was not discouraging qualified teachers. In fact, the Bible encourages the mature to teach (Hebrews 5:12–14). We must remember that not everyone is called to be a teacher. Sometimes "teachers" often misinform and mislead their listeners, who in turn misinform and mislead others (2 Peter 2:1–2). James warned that because teachers are responsible to their followers, they will be judged much more harshly for the errors they teach. The words we speak have a far deeper impact than we often realize. This is especially true in the body of the Church. The spiritual health of the congregation is much better off when the leaders and teachers of the Church, who use their speech to influence others, exercise spiritual maturity and godly control in this area. They must pray as David prayed, "I will take heed to my ways, that I sin not with my tongue" (from Psalm 39:1).

In chapter 1, James had warned that if our religion seems true but we are unable to control our speech, then our religion is in vain (verse 26). In the first illustration, James compared the tongue to a bit used to control a horse. In the second illustration, he compared the tongue to a ship's rudder.

Both the bit and the rudder are small objects used to steer and control something far larger. They are seemingly unimportant, but their purpose is critical. Without a bit in the horse's mouth, the rider cannot control the massive animal beneath him and turn the horse when necessary. Without a rudder, the ship would float aimlessly.

In these illustrations, James was pointing out the importance of our words and the power they contain. Our ability to control our speech is an indication of our ability to control our desires, most especially our desire to please God. Whether truth or lie, a compliment or an insult, our words can have a profound impact on our lives and on the lives of others. This power is too much for us to handle. In the same way the horse needs the bit in his mouth and the rider to control him, and the ship needs the captain at the helm and rudder to keep the ship's course, we need Christ to control our speech.

Discipline of the Tongue (verses 1–4)

1 My brethren, be not many masters, knowing that we shall receive the greater condemnation. 2 For in many things we offend all. If any man offend not in word, the same is a perfect man, and able also to bridle the whole body. 3 Behold, we put bits in the horses' mouths, that they may obey us; and we turn about their whole body. 4 Behold also the ships, which though they be so great, and are driven of fierce winds, yet are they turned about with a very small helm, whithersoever the governor listeth.

The Greek word *didaskaloi* (**did-AS-kal-oy**), translated in the King James Version as "masters," means also "teachers." The teachers in this context were Jewish males, including the author, James, with expert training in the Scriptures. As such, they were authority figures held in high esteem. Some people wanted to become teachers to attain higher social status. However, those trained in the Scriptures were also charged with imparting to the community how to live according to God's will. Therefore, they were held to a higher standard. If they led the believers astray, they would be judged (*Gk. krima* , **KREE-mah**) more harshly than others.

The Greek word for "offend" is *ptaio* (**PTAH-yo**) and means to stumble. James acknowledged that as human beings we too often get tripped up and do or say things we don't intend to. But the person who has the ability to guard his speech achieves perfection in disciplining his entire body. The Greek word for "perfect" (*teleios,* **TEL-i-os**), when referring to human beings, does not mean without sin. Rather, it symbolizes the attainment of a virtue in a moral sense. For example, we often hear that "patience is a virtue." Anyone who has worked with children knows that they can test one's patience. However, the person who is able to deal with children without complaining or losing control of his temper is considered perfect in this sense.

A "bridle" (Gk. *chalinagogeo* , **khal-in-ag-OGUEEH-o**) is literally a harness that fits over a horse's head. It has a bit that fits into the horse's mouth and reins that guide the animal in the direction it should go. Figuratively, to "bridle" one's speech means to show restraint.

Horses were a common mode of transportation in the first century. Roman soldiers also used them in battles. People who ride horses use a bridle to control or guide the horse's movement. The horse responds to the tugging on the bit in its mouth by turning its whole body in the direction its rider wants it to go. Likewise, when we demonstrate the ability to control our speech, we display the discipline to govern other members of our body and guide them in the direction they should go. James furthered his argument on the importance of selecting teachers who have mastered the ability to guard their speech (and therefore their whole bodies) by using the example of a ship at sea being steered by something as small as a rudder. The Greek verb *metago* (**met-AG-o**) means to guide, to turn about, or to change direction. Similar to the horse, a large ship, which needs the power of strong winds in order to move it, is able to be steered this way or that by such a small thing as the rudder (Gk. *pedalion* , **pay-DAL-ee-on**).

II . THE POWER OF WORDS
(James 3:5–6)

James moved on to show the destructive potential of the tongue by describing how something as
small as a "little fire" can rage out of control. This metaphor is especially meaningful to present-day believers who grew up with commercials stressing how a little match, when carelessly tossed away, could result in the destruction of an entire forest.

Destructiveness of the Tongue (verses 5–6)

5 Even so the tongue is a little member, and boasteth great things. Behold, how great a matter a little fire kindleth! 6 And the tongue is a fire, a world of iniquity: so is the tongue among our members, that it defileth the whole body, and setteth on fire the course of nature; and it is set on fire of hell. James finally got to the heart of his sermon: that something as small as the tongue (Gk. glossa, GLOCE-sah) can wield great power for good or evil. The forest fire metaphor is a good example of how a single spark can start a fire that can quickly burn out of control. If the right person is in control of speech, then he or she can guide others in the right way to go. Likewise, a single word by a person with no self-control can do damage that can take months or even years to repair.

James returned again to the metaphor of the tongue represented by the teacher within the community whose speech could bring good or evil to bear. This verse is obscure and many scholars have found it difficult to interpret. The world of first century Rome was far removed from our contemporary society, and many of the metaphors and images used in ancient writings such as the Bible are unfamiliar to today's readers. The Greek word for "iniquity," also called unrighteousness, is *adikia* (**ad-ee-KEE-ah**) and means a deed violating law and justice, as in an unfair judge. A biased judge who hands down an unjust ruling negatively impacts the individual, his or her family, and the whole community. Or the tongue, with its potential for sin, represents a smaller version of the potential for all of humanity to sin.

III. UNTAMEABLE (JAMES 3:7–8)

James now turned his attention to the

difficulty in trying to tame the tongue. While all manner of birds, animals, reptiles, and creatures of the sea could be tamed, the human tongue is more difficult to control. This is affirmed when we read, "He that keepeth his mouth keepeth his life: but he that openeth wide his lips shall have destruction" (Proverbs 13:3). Examples of thoughtless, careless, and unkind speech include profanity, lying, gossiping, disclosing things that are told to us in confidence, and guessing and speculating about matters

Defiance of the Tongue (verses 7–8)

7 For every kind of beasts, and of birds, and of serpents, and of things in the sea, is tamed, and hath been tamed of mankind. 8 But the tongue can no man tame; it is an unruly evil, full of deadly poison. James likened the tongue to a living being. However, in contrast to all the creatures of the land and sea which human beings are capable of restraining (Gk.*damazo*, dam-ad-ZO), humans appear to be incapable of taming the tongue.

We might believe that James exaggerated the power of the tongue by comparing it to fires raging out of control. However, he took very seriously the power of someone in the authority position of a teacher to do great harm if he does not have theability to control his speech. James referred to the tongue as "an unruly evil" (Gk. *kakon* , **kak-ON**).

In the Greco-Roman context of the first century, the word "evil" meant to be foul or rotten down to the bone. It was an inward decay, somewhatlike a cancer developing and spreading through one's body. Anyone who has ever been the victim of slander knows how lies left unchallenged can destroy careers and

lives.

IV. TWO -FACED OR FAITHFUL? (James 3:9–12)

James pointed out the perverse ability of man to "bless" God and "curse" men with the same mouth. If we use our mouths for bad, it taints our ability to use them for good. How effective can a parent be if he screams at his children and calls them "stupid" one day then tries to encourage them the next? Controlling our tongue is a constant and conscious effort. We have to be aware of it all day, every day.

Duplicity of the Tongue (verses 9–12)

9 Therewith bless we God, even the Father; and therewith curse we men, which are made after the similitude of God. 10 Out of the same mouth proceedeth blessing and cursing. My brethren, these things ought not so to be. 11 Doth a fountain send forth at the same place sweet water and bitter? 12 Can the fig tree, my brethren, bear olive berries? either a vine, figs? so can no fountain both yield salt water and fresh.

It is ironic that the very same tongue we use to bless God is also used to curse others. The Greek word for "bless," *eulogon* (**YOO-log-on**), is from the same root as the word "eulogy" and means good words. To bless someone is to speak well of them or to praise them. In contrast, "to curse" (Gk. *kataraomai*, **kat-ar-AH-om-ahee**) someone means to doom or call down evil upon him or her. As creatures made in the image and likeness (Gk.*homoiosis* , **hom-OY-o-sis**) of God, we should have only good words for one another.

The Greek word for "mouth," *stoma* (**STOM-a**), refers both to the opening on the edge of the lips through which food enters, and speech, especially eloquent speech. It also means the point on a sword. Metaphorically, the tongue can be a sharp sword cutting down people with insults and imprecations. Or it can offer words of praise that lift up people. The notion that both virtuous and vile speech can come from the same source was anathema to James. Fresh or living (Gk. *glukus,* **GLOO-koos,** literally "sweet") water is from a new or previously unused source. Bitter or brackish (Gk. *pikros,* **peek-ROS**) water is fresh water mixed with salt water, such as in river estuaries like Lake Pontchartrain in Louisiana. Living water is uncontaminated and refreshing; you wouldn't want to drink from brackish water that has not been treated to remove the salty taste. Those of us who grew up in urban areas have probably never encountered brackish water. However, those from rural areas likely learned as children not to drink such water. James rhetorically asked whether fresh and brackish water can come from the same source, knowing that his audience, who had come in contact with both types of water, would answer no.

Anyone who has ever cultivated or produced crops for food knows that a fig tree cannot yield olives any more than a grapevine can produce figs. This would be an aberration of nature. The fig tree can only produce figs and the olive tree only olives, as is their nature. Likewise, salt (Gk. *halykos,* **halyeek-OS**) water cannot yield sweet (fresh) water. James was making the point that a person with an evil disposition is not likely to be virtuous, as it is not in them to do so.

SEARCH THE SCRIPTURES
QUESTIONS

1. The tongue _____ God and _____ people.

2. James compares the believer's tongue that praises and curses with what in nature?

BIBLE APPLICATION

AIM: Students will understand the challenge of controlling the tongue and ask God for help.

What a wonderful gift speech is. Christians have the ability to exhort, coach, and build up other believers through our speech. Similarly, our words provide the vehicle to lovingly counsel the lost and to soothe and console the suffering and bereaved. This gift of speech is most perfectly employed when we speak words of truth and witness to others of God's saving plan. We must be very careful not to abuse this wonderful gift. Many Christians would never imagine causing someone physical harm. Yet this is exactly what we do when we say thoughtless, careless, and unkind things to or about others. We verbally murder the character and reputations of others when our speech is unrestrained. Each day offers us a challenge to not only walk in the will and the way of our Lord, but also to speak in ways that glorify Him and all of His creation.

STUDENTS ' RESPONSES

AIM: Students will make sure their walk and talk mirror those of Christ.

It's never easy to listen to someone say unfair, incorrect, or mean-spirited things to us. Yet as Christians, we are never allowed to respond in kind. Our obligation is always to show a dying world that we are the children of a living God. We can only do this when our walk and our talk mirror those of our Savior. What comes out of our mouths must be loving. This means that our motivation to speak must be godly and intended to comfort, heal, and teach godly principles to others. Pray, and ask God to use your speech as a vehicle for aid, comfort, and reconciliation.

PRAYER

Lord, we thank You that You do not count our sins against us. Thank You that there is forgiveness in the Name of your Son Jesus. We ask that You would make us more vigilant over the words that we say. Father, we pray that You would use our tongues to for building others up instead of tearing them down. In Jesus' Name we pray. Amen.

DIG A LITTLE DEEPER

Allow me to introduce you to a weapon of mass destruction. It is the tongue! One of the smallest organs in the body has the potential to do evil. It is a fire and a world of iniquity. James gave an analogy of the horse and how the owner was able to guide him not just with bits but he had to put pressure on his tongue. He warned that if we cannot control our speech our religion must be in vain. Jesus said in Matthew 4:4 that it is written, man shall not live by bread alone but by every word that proceedeth out of the mouth of God. Speaking the Word of God is the only way to experience supernatural results. The tongue is an incredibly powerful tool that can be used to build up or tear down. The words that we speak should give life and not death. They should bring hope and not discouragement. Perhaps we can control this unruly weapon, after all. But to do so will require constant attention to who it affects and how it will affect us. We must think before we speak because this little member is packed with blessings and curses.

HOW TO SAY IT

Similitude. si-**MI**-li-tood, -tyood.

Josephus. joe-**SEE**-fus.

PREPARE FOR NEXT SUNDAY

Read **Leviticus 19:18; Deuteronomy 6:4-9; Mark 12:28:34,** and study "The Greatest Commandment."

Sources:
Bauer, Walter, William F. Arndt, F. Wilbur Gingrich, and Frederick W. Danker. A Greek-English Lexicon of the New Testament and Other Early Christian Literature, Second Edition. Chicago: University of Chicago Press, 1979.
Bible Study Tools. www.BibleStudyTools.com. Bakers Evangelical Dictionary. "James." http://www.biblestudytools.com/dictionaries/bakers-evangelical-dictionary/James-theology (accessed October 1, 2012).
Davids, Peter H. The Epistle of James. The New International Greek Testament Commentary. Grand Rapids, MI: Wm. B. Eerdmans Publishing Company, 1982.
Got Questions Ministries. "Book of James." http://www.gotquestions.org/Book-of-James.html (accessed October 2, 2012).
HarperCollins Study Bible (NRSV). New York: Harper Collins Publishers, 2006. 2052–2058.

DAILY HOME BIBLE READINGS

MONDAY
Lying and Flattering Lips
(Psalm 12)

TUESDAY
Words that Intimidate
(1 Samuel 17:1–11)

WEDNESDAY
Words that Lead to Repentance
(2 Chronicles 15:1–12)

THURSDAY
Words that Lead to Mourning
(Nehemiah 1)

FRIDAY
Words that Lead to Worship
(Genesis 24:42–52)

SATURDAY
Words Guided by Wisdom
(Proverbs 18:2–13)

SUNDAY
Taming the Tongue
(James 3:1–12)

The Symbol of the Church Of God In Christ

The Symbol of the Church Of God In Christ is an outgrowth of the Presiding Bishop's Coat of Arms, which has become quite familiar to the Church. The design of the Official Seal of the Church was created in 1973 and adopted in the General Assembly in 1981 (July Session).

The obvious GARNERED WHEAT in the center of the seal represents all of the people of the Church Of God In Christ, Inc. The ROPE of wheat that holds the shaft together represents the Founding Father of the Church, Bishop Charles Harrison Mason, who, at the call of the Lord, banded us together as a Brotherhood of Churches in the First Pentecostal General Assembly of the Church, in 1907.

The date in the seal has a two-fold purpose: first, to tell us that Bishop Mason received the baptism of the Holy Ghost in March 1907 and, second, to tell us that it was because of this outpouring that Bishop Mason was compelled to call us together in February of 1907 to organize the Church Of God In Christ.

The RAIN in the background represents the Latter Rain, or the End-time Revivals, which brought about the emergence of our Church along with other Pentecostal Holiness Bodies in the same era. The rain also serves as a challenge to the Church to keep Christ in the center of our worship and service, so that He may continue to use the Church Of God In Christ as one of the vehicles of Pentecostal Revival before the return of the Lord.

This information was reprinted from the book *So You Want to KNOW YOUR CHURCH* by Alferd Z. Hall, Jr.

COGIC AFFIRMATION OF FAITH

We believe the Bible to be the inspired and only infallible written Word of God.

We believe that there is One God, eternally existent in three Persons: God the Father, God the Son, and God the Holy Spirit.

We believe in the Blessed Hope, which is the rapture of the Church of God, which is in Christ at His return.

We believe that the only means of being cleansed from sin is through repentance and faith in the precious Blood of Jesus Christ.

We believe that regeneration by the Holy Ghost is absolutely essential for personal salvation.

We believe that the redemptive work of Christ on the Cross provides healing for the human body in answer to believing in prayer.

We believe that the baptism in the Holy Ghost, according to Acts 2:4, is given to believers who ask for it.

We believe in the sanctifying power of the Holy Spirit, by whose indwelling the Christian is enabled to live a Holy and separated life in this present world. Amen.

The Doctrines of the Church Of God In Christ

THE BIBLE

We believe that the Bible is the Word of God and contains one harmonious and sufficiently complete system of doctrine. We believe in the full inspiration of the Word of God. We hold the Word of God to be the only authority in all matters and assert that no doctrine can be true or essential if it does not find a place in this Word.

THE FATHER

We believe in God, the Father Almighty, the Author and Creator of all things. The Old Testament reveals God in diverse manners, by manifesting His nature, character, and dominions. The Gospels in the New Testament give us knowledge of God the "Father" or "My Father," showing the relationship of God to Jesus as Father, or representing Him as the Father in the Godhead, and Jesus himself that Son (St. John 15:8, 14:20). Jesus also gives God the distinction of "Fatherhood" to all believers when He explains God in the light of "Your Father in Heaven" (St. Matthew 6:8).

THE SON

We believe that Jesus Christ is the Son of God, the second person in the Godhead of the Trinity or Triune Godhead. We believe that Jesus was and is eternal in His person and nature as the Son of God who was with God in the beginning of creation (St. John 1:1). We believe that Jesus Christ was born of a virgin called Mary according to the Scripture (St. Matthew 1:18), thus giving rise to our fundamental belief in the Virgin Birth and to all of the miraculous events surrounding the phenomenon (St. Matthew 1:18–25). We believe that Jesus Christ became the "suffering servant" to man; this suffering servant came seeking to redeem man from sin and to reconcile him to God, his Father (Romans 5:10). We believe that Jesus Christ is standing now as mediator between God and man (I Timothy 2:5).

THE HOLY GHOST

We believe the Holy Ghost or Holy Spirit is the third person of the Trinity; proceeds from the Father and the Son; is of the same substance, equal to power and glory; and is together with the Father and the Son, to be believed in, obeyed, and worshiped. The Holy Ghost is a gift bestowed upon the believer for the purpose of equipping and empowering the believer, making him or her a more effective witness for service in the world. He teaches and guides one into all truth (John 16:13; Acts 1:8, 8:39).

THE BAPTISM OF THE HOLY GHOST

We believe that the Baptism of the Holy Ghost is an experience subsequent to conversion and sanctification and that tongue-speaking is the consequence of the baptism in the Holy Ghost with the manifestations of the fruit of the spirit (Galatians 5:22–23; Acts 10:46, 19:1–6). We believe that we are not baptized with the Holy Ghost in order to be saved (Acts 19:1–6; John 3:5). When one receives a baptismal Holy Ghost experience, we believe one will speak with a tongue unknown to oneself according to the sovereign will of Christ. To be filled with the Spirit means to be Spirit controlled as expressed by Paul in Ephesians 5:18,19. Since the charismatic demonstrations were necessary to help the early church to be successful in implementing the command of Christ, we, therefore, believe that a Holy Ghost experience is mandatory for all believers today.

MAN

We believe that humankind was created holy by God, composed of body, soul, and spirit. We believe that humankind, by nature, is sinful and unholy. Being born in sin, a person needs to be born again, sanctified and cleansed from all sins by the blood of Jesus. We believe that one is saved by confessing and forsaking one's sins, and believing on the Lord Jesus Christ, and that having become a child of God, by being born again and adopted into the family of God, one may, and should, claim the inheritance of the sons of God, namely the baptism of the Holy Ghost.

SIN

Sin, the Bible teaches, began in the angelic world (Ezekiel 28:11–19; Isaiah 14:12–20) and is transmitted into the blood of the human race through disobedience and deception motivated by unbelief (I Timothy 2:14). Adam's sin, committed by eating of the forbidden fruit from the tree of knowledge of good and evil, carried with it permanent pollution or depraved human nature to all his descendants. This is called "original sin." Sin can now be defined as a volitional transgression against God and a lack of conformity to the will of God. We, therefore, conclude that humankind by nature is sinful and has fallen from a glorious and righteous state from which we were created, and has become unrighteous and unholy.

We therefore, must be restored to the state of holiness from which we have fallen by being born again (St. John 3:7).

SALVATION

Salvation deals with the application of the work of redemption to the sinner with restoration to divine favor and communion with God. This redemptive operation of the Holy Ghost upon sinners is brought about by repentance toward God and faith toward our Lord Jesus Christ which brings conversion, faith, justification, regeneration, sanctification, and the baptism of the Holy Ghost. Repentance is the work of God, which results in a change of mind in respect to a person's relationship to God (St. Matthew 3:1–2, 4:17; Acts 20:21). Faith is a certain conviction wrought in the heart by the Holy Spirit, as to the truth of the Gospel and a heart trust in the promises of God in Christ (Romans 1:17, 3:28; St. Matthew 9:22; Acts 26:18). Conversion is that act of God whereby He causes the regenerated sinner, in one's conscious life, to turn to Him in repentance and faith (II Kings 5:15; II Chronicles 33:12,13; St. Luke 19:8,9; Acts 8:30). Regeneration is the act of God by which the principle of the new life is implanted in humankind, the governing disposition of soul is made holy, and the first holy exercise of this new disposition is secured. Sanctification is that gracious and continuous operation of the Holy Ghost, by which He delivers the justified sinner from the pollution of sin, renews a person's whole nature in the image of God, and enables one to perform good works (Romans 6:4, 5:6; Colossians 2:12, 3:1).

ANGELS

The Bible uses the term "angel" (a heavenly body) clearly and primarily to denote messengers or ambassadors of God with such Scripture references as Revelations 4:5, which indicates their duty in heaven to praise God (Psalm 103:20), to do God's will (St. Matthew 18:10), and to behold His face. But since heaven must come down to earth, they also have a mission to earth. The Bible indicates that they accompanied God in the Creation, and also that they will accompany Christ in His return in Glory.

DEMONS

Demons denote unclean or evil spirits; they are sometimes called devils or demonic beings. They are evil spirits, belonging to the unseen or spiritual realm, embodied in human beings. The Old Testament refers to the prince of demons, sometimes called Satan (adversary) or Devil, as having power and wisdom, taking the habitation of other forms such as the serpent (Genesis 3:1). The New Testament speaks of the Devil as Tempter (St. Matthew 4:3), and it goes on to tell the works of Satan, the Devil, and demons as combating righteousness and good in any form, proving to be an adversary to the saints. Their chief power is exercised to destroy the mission of Jesus Christ. It can well be said that the Christian Church believes in demons, Satan, and devils. We believe in their power and purpose. We believe they can be subdued and conquered as in the commandment to the believer by Jesus. "In my name they shall cast out Satan and the work of the Devil and to resist him and then he will flee (WITHDRAW) from you" (St. Mark 16:17).

THE CHURCH

The Church forms a spiritual unity of which Christ is the divine head. It is animated by one Spirit, the Spirit of Christ. It professes one faith, shares one hope, and serves one King. It is the citadel of the truth and God's agency for communicating to believers all spiritual blessings. The Church then is the object of our faith rather than of knowledge. The name of our Church, "CHURCH OF GOD IN CHRIST," is supported by I Thessalonians 2:14 and other passages in the Pauline Epistles. The word "CHURCH" or "EKKLESIA" was first applied to the Christian society by Jesus Christ in St. Matthew 16:18, the occasion being that of His benediction of Peter at Caesarea Philippi.

THE SECOND COMING OF CHRIST

We believe in the second coming of Christ; that He shall come from heaven to earth, personally, bodily, visibly (Acts 1:11; Titus 2:11–13; St. Matthew 16:27, 24:30, 25:30; Luke 21:27; John 1:14, 17; Titus 2:11); and that the Church, the bride, will be caught up to meet Him in the air (I Thessalonians 4:16–17). We admonish all who have this hope to purify themselves as He is pure.

DIVINE HEALING

The Church Of God In Christ believes in and practices Divine Healing. It is a commandment of Jesus to the Apostles (St. Mark 16:18). Jesus affirms His teachings on healing by explaining to His disciples, who were to be Apostles, that healing the afflicted is by faith (St. Luke 9:40–41). Therefore, we believe that healing by faith in God has scriptural support and ordained authority. St. James's writings in his epistle encourage Elders to pray for the sick, lay hands upon them and to anoint them with oil, and state that prayers with faith shall heal the sick and the Lord shall raise them up. Healing is still practiced widely and frequently in the Church Of God In Christ, and testimonies of healing in our Church testify to this fact.

MIRACLES

The Church Of God In Christ believes that miracles occur to convince people that the Bible is God's Word. A miracle can be defined as an extraordinary visible act of divine power, wrought by the efficient agency of the will of God, which has as its final cause the vindication of the righteousness of God's Word. We believe that the works of God, which were performed during the beginnings of Christianity, do and will occur even today where God is preached, faith in Christ is exercised, the Holy Ghost is active, and the Gospel is promulgated in the truth (Acts 5:15, 6:8, 9:40; Luke 4:36, 7:14, 15, 5:5, 6; St. Mark 14:15).

THE ORDINANCES OF THE CHURCH

It is generally admitted that for an ordinance to be valid, it must have been instituted by Christ. When we speak of ordinances of the church, we are speaking of those instituted by Christ, in which by sensible signs the grace of God in Christ and the benefits of the covenant of grace are represented, sealed, and applied to believers, and these in turn give expression to their faith and allegiance to God. The Church Of God In Christ recognizes three ordinances as having been instituted by Christ himself and, therefore, are binding upon the church practice.

THE LORD'S SUPPER (HOLY COMMUNION)

The Lord's Supper symbolizes the Lord's death and suffering for the benefit and in the place of His people. It also symbolizes the believer's participation in the crucified Christ. It represents not only the death of Christ as the object of faith, which unites the believers to Christ, but also the effect of this act as the giving of life, strength, and joy to the soul. The communicant by faith enters into a special spiritual union of one's soul with the glorified Christ.

FOOT WASHING

Foot washing is practiced and recognized as an ordinance in our Church because Christ, by His example, showed that humility characterized greatness in the kingdom of God, and that service rendered to others gave evidence that humility, motivated by love, exists. These services are held subsequent to the Lord's Supper; however, its regularity is left to the discretion of the pastor in charge.

WATER BAPTISM

We believe that Water Baptism is necessary as instructed by Christ in St. John 3:5, "UNLESS MAN BE BORN AGAIN OF WATER AND OF THE SPIRIT..."

However, we do not believe that water baptism alone is a means of salvation, but is an outward demonstration that one has already had a conversion experience and has accepted Christ as his personal Savior. As Pentecostals, we practice immersion in preference to sprinkling because immersion corresponds more closely to the death, burial, and resurrection of our Lord (Colossians 2:12). It also symbolizes regeneration and purification more than any other mode. Therefore, we practice immersion as our mode of baptism. We believe that we should use the Baptismal Formula given to us by Christ for all "...IN THE NAME OF THE FATHER, AND OF THE SON, AND OF THE HOLY GHOST..." (Matthew 28:19).

1. Call to order.

2. Singing.

3. Prayer.

4. **New Responsive Reading & Core Values**

ISSD: Responsive Reading

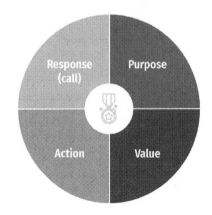

Calls for the response of worship of God
Calls for response to God (in unity)
Calls for response to God's truth

Builds identity around our core values
Builds student belief in themselves and in the mission of The Church

- To support students in achieving the curricular outcomes
- To inspire students to become engaged in comprehension and practice of scriptural commands

- For the life of The Church, it is:
  -biblical
  -historic
  -participatory
  -instructional

Responsive reading continued:

Sunday School's Core Values

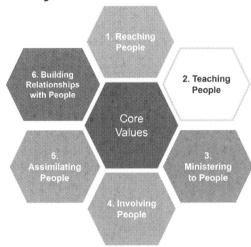

Core Values in Detail

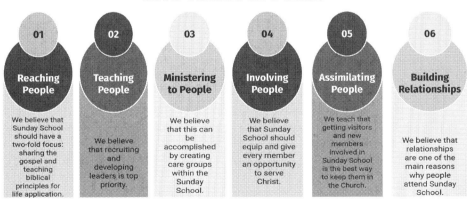

SUGGESTED ORDER OF SERVICE

SUPERINTENDENT/TEACHER: Behold how good and how pleasant it is for brethren to dwell together in unity! *Psalm 133:1*

SCHOOL/CLASS: But to do good and to communicate forget not: for with such sacrifices God is well pleased. *Hebrews 13:16*

SUPERINTENDENT/TEACHER: All scripture is given by inspiration of God, and is profitable for doctrine, for reproof, for correction, for instruction in righteousness. *2 Timothy 3:16*

SCHOOL/CLASS: Thy word is a lamp unto my feet, and a light unto my path. *Psalm 119:105*

SUPERINTENDENT/TEACHER: Look not every man on his own things, but every man also on the things of others. *Philippians 2:4*

SCHOOL/CLASS: He that hath a bountiful eye shall be blessed; for he giveth of his bread to the poor. *Proverbs 22:9*

SUPERINTENDENT/TEACHER: Wherefore he saith, When he ascended up on high, he led captivity captive, and gave gifts unto men. *Ephesians 4:8*

SCHOOL/CLASS: As every man hath received the gift, even so minister the same one to another, as good stewards of the manifold grace of God. *1 Peter 4:10*

SUPERINTENDENT/TEACHER: For as the body is one, and hath many members, and all the members of that one body, being many, are one body: so also is Christ. *1 Corinthians 12:12*

SCHOOL/CLASS: For as we have many members in one body, and all members have not the same office. *Romans 12:4*

SUPERINTENDENT/TEACHER: By this shall all men know that ye are my disciples, if ye have love one to another. *John 13:35*

SCHOOL/CLASS: For, brethren, ye have been called unto liberty for an occasion to the flesh, but by love serve one another. *Galatians 5:13*

SUPERINTENDENT/ALL: But grow in grace, and in the knowledge of our Lord and Savior Jesus Christ. To him be glory both now and for ever. Amen. *2 Peter 3:18*

5. Singing.
6. Reading lesson by school and superintendent.
7. Classes assemble for lesson study.
8. Sunday School offering.
9. Five-minute warning bell.
10. Closing bell.
11. Brief lesson review by pastor or superintendent.
12. Secretary's report.
13. Announcements.
14. Dismissal.

Notes

Notes

Notes

Notes

Notes

Notes